W. B. YEATS

THE TOWER (1928)

A FACSIMILE EDITION

WITH AN INTRODUCTION AND NOTES
BY

RICHARD J. FINNERAN

SCRIBNER
NEW YORK   LONDON   TORONTO   SYDNEY

SCRIBNER
1230 Avenue of the Americas
New York, NY 10020

First Scribner trade paperback edition 2004

SCRIBNER and design are trademarks of Macmillan Library Reference USA, Inc.,
used under license by Simon & Schuster, the publisher of this work.

For information about special discounts for bulk purchases,
please contact Simon & Schuster Special Sales:
1-800-456-6798 or business@simonandschuster.com

DESIGNED BY ERICH HOBBING

Text set in Scotch Roman

Manufactured in the United States of America

5   7   9   10   8   6

Library of Congress Cataloging-in-Publication Data
Yeats, W. B. (William Butler), 1865–1939.
The tower : a facsimile edition / W. B. Yeats ; with an introduction and notes
by Richard J. Finneran.—1st Scribner trade pbk. ed.
p.   cm.
I. Finneran, Richard J. II. Title.
PR5904.T6 2004
821'.8—dc22   2003065187

ISBN-13: 978-0-7432-4728-3
ISBN-10:   0-7432-4728-0

CONTENTS

PREFACE   VII

INTRODUCTION   IX

THE TOWER (1928)   1

NOTES TO YEATS'S NOTES   111

NOTES TO THE POEMS   115

PREFACE

This edition offers a facsimile of the first London edition of *The Tower,* published by Macmillan on 14 February 1928. The copy used is that in the Wilson Library, University of North Carolina at Chapel Hill (PR5904.T6 1928 Copy 1). This edition also offers an introduction that traces the production of the 1928 volume and the later revisions as well as annotations to Yeats's Notes and editorial notes to each poem.

I am grateful to George Bornstein of the University of Michigan and Charles B. McNamara of the Wilson Library at the University of North Carolina at Chapel Hill for their suggestions and to Sarah McGrath of Scribner for her support of this project. I am also indebted to John McGhee for his careful work in seeing the volume through the press.

This edition is dedicated to Nora FitzGerald.

R.J.F.
Wildwood, Missouri
19 July 2002

INTRODUCTION

A last-minute shopper entering a London bookstore on Valentine's Day in 1928 with six shillings to spend on a gift for his or her beloved could hardly have made a better investment—either poetically or financially—than one of the 2,000 copies of a volume Macmillan & Co. had published that morning: *The Tower* by W. B. Yeats. Twenty-one poems in 104 pages; six pages of notes; olive green cloth with a design by T. Sturge Moore stamped in gold on front and spine, also reproduced on the dust jacket. No illustrations, no book club dividends: simply one of the seminal volumes of Modern Poetry, indeed of poetry in English as we know it. Doubtless not every lyric is a masterpiece, but how often have we been given between two covers such "monuments of magnificence" as "Sailing to Byzantium," "Leda and the Swan," and "Among School Children"—not to mention "The Tower," "Meditations in Time of Civil War," "Nineteen Hundred and Nineteen," or "Two Songs from a Play"? "A thing never known again," indeed.[1]

The gestation of *The Tower* was a long process. A draft of "The New Faces" was sent to Lady Gregory on 7 December 1912; a draft of "From 'Oedipus at Colonus'" was sent to Olivia Shakespear on 13 March 1927. Yeats began to publish the poems that would form *The Tower*

in journals as early as March 1921 and in book form the following year: *Seven Poems and a Fragment,* an edition of only 500 copies by the Cuala Press, the private press run by his sisters. Two more Cuala Press volumes would follow—*The Cat and the Moon and Certain Poems* (1924), again in a printing of only 500 copies; and *October Blast* (1927), one of the rarest of all Cuala publications, only 350 copies. The single poem in *The Tower* not previously published would be "Colonus' Praise." Finally, on 16 September 1927, Yeats submitted copy for the volume to Macmillan:

> I send you . . . the manuscript of 'The Tower.' Feeling that it was exaggerated in certain directions I continually put off sending it, but I cannot delay any longer. If, when you have received the Manuscript, you think the book too small, or have any fault to find, please delay it for a few months.

Yeats went on to explain that he was writing a series of poems for a limited American edition (*The Winding Stair,* 1929) and that these could be added to *The Tower* in a year. Seldom has a Nobel Laureate been quite so diffident about his latest work.

Although the Cuala Press *Michael Robartes and the Dancer* (1921) had been included in *Later Poems* (1922), Macmillan had not published a major new volume of Yeats's poetry since *The Wild Swans at Coole* (1919). It is thus not surprising that the publisher gave little heed to Yeats's reservations about *The Tower* and instead put the book into production, with publication on 14 February

1928. The volume quickly sold out, and a second impression was issued in March. In July 1929 Macmillan published a third impression with some corrections. An edition by Macmillan, New York, appeared on 22 May 1928, with a second impression in January 1929.[2]

As usual, Yeats treated *The Tower* as a unique work, not simply a collection of poems. The order of the poems was anything but chronological, either in terms of composition or of the events depicted. For instance, the second poem written and the first published, "All Souls' Night," was placed last. "Meditations in Time of Civil War," describing the violence in Ireland of 1922–23, precedes "Nineteen Hundred and Nineteen." A poem that concludes with the story of Christ, "Two Songs from a Play," is followed by one that describes the union of Leda and Zeus.

Yeats's interest in *The Tower* as a separate work of art extended to the physical book itself. Once the arrangements for the volume had been made with Macmillan, he enlisted his friend T. Sturge Moore, a writer and artist, to undertake the design, writing him on 23 May 1927:

> I want you to design the cover—design in gold—and a frontispiece. The book is to be called *The Tower,* as a number of the poems were written at and about Ballylee Castle. The frontispiece I want is a drawing of the castle, something of the nature of a woodcut. If you consent I will send you a bundle of photographs. It is a most impressive building and what I want is an imaginative impression. Do what you like with cloud and bird, day and night, but leave the great walls as they are.[3]

Moore immediately agreed. Yeats sent him some poems and photographs and made the further suggestion that "the Tower should not be too unlike the real object, or rather that it should suggest the real object. I like to think of that building as a permanent symbol of my work plainly visible to the passer-by. As you know, all my art theories depend upon just this—rooting of mythology in the earth" (*LTSM* 114).[4] Yeats approved of Moore's design of the Tower reflected in the adjacent stream, telling him, "It is interesting that you should have completed Tower symbolism by surrounding it with water" (*LTSM* 111). Unfortunately, because of some lost or misdirected correspondence, Moore failed to produce a frontispiece. But when Yeats received a copy of the volume, he wrote Moore from Rapallo on 23 February 1928, "Your cover for *The Tower* is a most rich, grave and beautiful design, admirably like the place . . ." (*LTSM* 123).

Yeats's earliest recorded comment on the book as a whole was made in a letter to Lady Gregory on 24 March 1928: "*The Tower* astonishes me by its bitterness."[5] On 25 April 1928 he told Olivia Shakespear, "Re-reading *The Tower* I was astonished at its bitterness, and long to live out of Ireland that I may find some new vintage. Yet that bitterness gave the book its power and it is the best book I have written."[6]

Although there was the odd dissenting voice, by and large the reviewers were in accord with Yeats's judgment on his achievement. Writing to Yeats less than two weeks after publication, Lennox Robinson commented that "'The Tower' seems to be getting wonderful notices, the Observer has it as a 'best seller'. . . . and the Independent

this morning is extraordinarily intelligent."[7] Yeats himself told Lady Gregory on 1 April 1928 that "*Tower* is receiving great favour. Perhaps the reviewers know that I am so ill that I can be commended without future inconvenience. . . . Even the Catholic Press is enthusiastic" (*L* 740). Likewise, he wrote Olivia Shakespear on 25 April 1928, "*The Tower* is a great success, two thousand copies in the first month, much the largest sale I have ever had . . ." (*L* 742). In an unsigned review in *The Times Literary Supplement* for 1 March 1928, for example, Austin Clarke found in *The Tower* "a freedom of the poetic elements, an imaginative and prosodic beauty that brings one the pure and impersonal joy of art"; he also praised "the delightful cover design of this book." Writing in *The Criterion* for September 1928, John Gould Fletcher offered *The Tower* as evidence that Yeats "corresponds, or will correspond, when the true literary history of our epoch is written, to what we moderns mean by a great poet." In *The New Republic* for 10 October 1928 Theodore Spencer noted that "on the whole, the poems in this book are among the finest Mr. Yeats has written" and that "many . . . will remain a permanent part of English poetry." In sum, the consensus of both the reviewers and most later critics and readers of Yeats's poetry is well represented by Virginia Woolf's judgment in an unsigned review in *The Nation & Athenaeum* for 21 April 1928: "Mr. Yeats has never written more exactly and more passionately."

Most other poets would have been more than content with such acclaim, and the story of *The Tower* would

have ended. But Yeats as usual was not content, and over the next five years he would make significant changes to the volume, so much so that readers who know *The Tower* only from its final version will find this facsimile edition more than a little surprising.

For the 1929 third impression Yeats made only minor changes, some as small—but telling—as the addition of a hyphen in "moon-luminous" ("Meditations in Time of Civil War," III.10), some more significant, such as that to lines 5–6 of "Sailing to Byzantium." The text in 1928 is virtually unpronounceable:

> Fish flesh or fowl, commend all summer long
> Whatever is begotten born and dies.

One is tempted to think that both Yeats and the proof-reader at Macmillan had nodded off, but in fact the exact same version had appeared a year earlier in *October Blast,* and on the proofs of that volume Yeats made a correction elsewhere in the first stanza of the poem but left these lines untouched. A second version appeared when the poem was used as the epigraph in *Stories of Red Hanrahan and The Secret Rose* (1927):

> Fish, flesh or fowl, commend all summer long
> Whatever is begotten born and dies.

This is arguably worse, and one is again tempted to assume somnolence. However, on 10 September 1927 Yeats had written Macmillan, "I return the proof of the poem, which is now correct. Through vacillation over

the punctuation of the first stanza I have made a blotted proof but I think it is clear."[8] So it was not until the 1929 version of *The Tower* that we are offered what surely seems the inevitable version (even if grammarians would protest the comma after "fowl"):

> Fish, flesh, or fowl, commend all summer long
> Whatever is begotten, born, and dies.

Yeats's next opportunity to revise *The Tower* occurred in connection with the volume of *Poems* in the Edition de Luxe, a project that in the event would never see the light of day. Either when he submitted copy on 1 June 1931 or when he corrected two sets of proofs from June through September 1932, Yeats made only one change of note, but it is an important one: "From 'Oedipus at Colonus'" was removed from its placement after "The Three Monuments" and was now included as section XI of "A Man Young and Old." As the new conclusion to the sequence, the choral ode, with its celebration of "the silent kiss that ends short life or long" and its invocation of "a gay goodnight," ameliorates, or at least puts into a changed perspective, the "bitterness" of the original ending, in which the speaker lamented that "Being all alone I'd nurse a stone / And sing it lullaby."

With the Edition de Luxe in limbo, Yeats suggested to his publishers that they should bring out a regular edition of a *Collected Poems,* and they agreed. This provided another opportunity to revise *The Tower,* and Yeats did not fail to seize it. The most visible change of all was the removal of "The Gift of Harun Al-Rashid" to the "Nar-

rative and Dramatic" section at the end of the book, where it became the final poem in the volume. In a letter of 30 March 1933, Macmillan had suggested such a two-part division for the new collection and had listed five candidates for the second section. Yeats quickly indicated that he was "delighted" with the proposal. "The Gift of Harun-Al-Rashid" had not been on Macmillan's list, but it was nevertheless absent from *The Tower* when the *Collected Poems* was published in London on 28 November 1933, in an edition of 2,040 copies. Whether this was based on a later suggestion by Macmillan or was Yeats's own idea is unknown. (My guess is the latter.) In any case, Yeats in effect replaced "The Gift of Harun Al-Rashid" with the inclusion of an entirely new poem, "Fragments": part I had been published in an essay in the *Dublin Magazine* for October–December 1931; part II was taken from a draft of the Introduction to *The Resurrection*. From a biographical perspective, "The Gift of Harun Al-Rashid" is a veiled tribute to the automatic writing and other activities by Mrs. W. B. Yeats that produced the materials for *A Vision* (1925). Its placement at the end of the *Collected Poems* was thus altogether appropriate. "Fragments" is a fanciful epitome of the longer poem, with Mrs. Yeats quite literally the "medium" who provided Yeats with the "truth" that *A Vision* would present:

I

Locke sank into a swoon;
The Garden died;
God took the spinning-jenny
Out of his side.

II

Where got I that truth?
Out of a medium's mouth,
Out of nothing it came,
Out of the forest loam,
Out of dark night where lay
The crowns of Nineveh. (*P* 217–18)

Yeats situated "Fragments" in a rather important position, between "Two Songs from a Play" and "Leda and the Swan," displacing "Wisdom" to follow "Colonus' Praise." He made two other major changes to *The Tower*: he added to "Two Songs from a Play" a fourth stanza, first published in *Stories of Michael Robartes and His Friends* (1932); and he deleted the first seventeen lines of "The Hero, the Girl, and the Fool," printing the final ten lines as "The Fool by the Roadside," the form used in *A Vision* (1925).[9]

Yeats had one more opportunity to revise *The Tower*, in June 1937 when he submitted copy for another never-to-be-published project, the Scribner Edition; but for once he restrained himself.[10] Thus from 1933 onward, *The Tower* was understood to be the form included in the *Collected Poems*. It is a fundamentally different volume from that first published. This present edition allows readers access to the original version, with unadorned texts and only the handful of Notes provided by Yeats. Perhaps it will also enable us to imagine how someone opening the pages of *The Tower* for the first time on Valentine's Day in 1928 would have received the masterful poems therein.

NOTES TO
THE INTRODUCTION

This essay draws on my " 'From things becoming to the thing become': The Construction of W. B. Yeats's *The Tower*," *South Atlantic Review* 63:1 (Winter 1998), 35–55.

1. "Beautiful Lofty Things," *The Poems,* 2nd edition, ed. Richard J. Finneran (New York: Scribner, 1997), 309. Hereafter cited as *P.*

2. The cover design of the New York edition was printed incorrectly, so that there are only three horizontal bars at the bottom and both "TSM DEL" and "The Macmillan Company" are omitted. The dust jacket was printed properly.

3. *W. B. Yeats and T. Sturge Moore: Their Correspondence 1901–1937,* ed. Ursula Bridge (London: Routledge & Kegan Paul, 1953), 109. Hereafter cited as *LTSM.* It is evident that some of the letters in this section of the edition are misdated and/or misordered.

4. He wrote on the reverse of one the photographs, "The cottage at back is my kitchen. In front you will see one parapet of the old bridge, the other was blown up during our civil war." *T. Sturge Moore (1870-1944): Contributions to the Art of the Book & Collaboration with Yeats,* compiled and ed. Malcolm Easton (Hull, England: University of Hull, 1970), 41.

5. *Letters of W. B. Yeats,* ed. Allan Wade (London: Rupert Hart-Davis, 1954), 738. Hereafter cited as *L.*

6. *L* 742. Likewise, the day before his letter to Lady Gregory just quoted, Yeats had written Olivia Shakespear, "Once

out of Irish bitterness I can find some measure of sweetness and of light—already new poems are floating in my head, bird songs of an old man, joy in the passing moment, emotion without the bitterness of memory" (*L* 737).

7. *Letters to W. B. Yeats,* ed. Richard J. Finneran, George Mills Harper, and William M. Murphy (London: Macmillan, 1977), vol. 2, 483.

8. British Library Add. Ms. 55003, f. 100. The same version appears in *The Exile* for spring 1928, although with the reading "born or dies," which almost surely is a misprint.

9. The new stanza of "Two Songs from a Play" is included in the editorial note to the poem (p. 121).

10. He would, however, revise lines 44–45 of "All Souls' Night" for the 1937 version of *A Vision*: "And knowing that the future would be vexed / With 'minished beauty, multiplied commonplace" becomes "And by foreknowledge of the future vexed; / Diminished beauty, multiplied commonplace." Not a model for grammarians, perhaps, but the revision eliminates both the ambiguity of the original and the rather awkward (to put it mildly) "'minished."

THE TOWER

MACMILLAN AND CO., Limited
LONDON · BOMBAY · CALCUTTA · MADRAS
MELBOURNE

THE MACMILLAN COMPANY
NEW YORK · BOSTON · CHICAGO
DALLAS · SAN FRANCISCO

THE MACMILLAN CO. OF CANADA, Ltd.
TORONTO

THE TOWER

BY

W. B. YEATS

MACMILLAN AND CO., LIMITED
ST. MARTIN'S STREET, LONDON
1928

PRINTED IN GREAT BRITAIN
BY R. & R. CLARK, LIMITED, EDINBURGH

CONTENTS

	PAGE
SAILING TO BYZANTIUM	1
THE TOWER	4
MEDITATIONS IN TIME OF CIVIL WAR	16
NINETEEN HUNDRED AND NINETEEN	32
THE WHEEL	42
YOUTH AND AGE	43
THE NEW FACES	44
A PRAYER FOR MY SON	45
TWO SONGS FROM A PLAY	47
WISDOM	49
LEDA AND THE SWAN	51
ON A PICTURE OF A BLACK CENTAUR	53
AMONG SCHOOL CHILDREN	55
COLONUS' PRAISE	61
THE HERO, THE GIRL, AND THE FOOL	64
OWEN AHERN AND HIS DANCERS	67
A MAN YOUNG AND OLD	70

v

vi　　　　**CONTENTS**

		PAGE
THE THREE MONUMENTS	. . .	79
FROM 'OEDIPUS AT COLONUS'	. .	80
THE GIFT OF HARUN AL-RASHID	. .	82
ALL SOULS' NIGHT	. . . .	98
NOTES .	. . . . .	105

SAILING TO BYZANTIUM

I

THAT is no country for old men.   The
    young
In one another's arms, birds in the
    trees,
—Those dying generations—at their
    song,
The   salmon - falls,   the   mackerel -
    crowded seas,
Fish   flesh   or   fowl,   commend   all
    summer long
Whatever is begotten born and dies.
Caught in that sensual music all neglect
Monuments of unaging intellect.

II

An aged man is but a paltry thing,
A tattered coat upon a stick, unless

Soul clap its hands and sing, and louder
    sing
For every tatter in its mortal dress,
Nor is there singing school but study-
    ing
Monuments of its own magnificence ;
And therefore I have sailed the seas
    and come
To the holy city of Byzantium.

III

O sages standing in God's holy fire
As in the gold mosaic of a wall,
Come from the holy fire, perne in a
    gyre,
And be the singing masters of my soul.
Consume my heart away ; sick with
    desire
And fastened to a dying animal
It knows not what it is ; and gather
    me
Into the artifice of eternity.

IV

Once out of nature I shall never take
My bodily form from any natural
    thing,
But such a form as Grecian gold-
    smiths make
Of hammered gold and gold enamelling
To keep a drowsy emperor awake ;
Or set upon a golden bough to sing
To lords and ladies of Byzantium
Of what is past, or passing, or to come.

1927

THE TOWER

WHAT shall I do with this absurdity—
O heart, O troubled heart—this cari-
    cature,
Decrepit age that has been tied to me
As to a dog's tail?

                Never had I more
Excited, passionate, fantastical
Imagination, nor an ear and eye
That more expected the impossible—
No, not in boyhood when with rod
    and fly,
Or the humbler worm, I climbed Ben
    Bulben's back
And had the livelong summer day to
    spend.

4

It seems that I must bid the Muse go
    pack,
Choose Plato and Plotinus for a friend
Until imagination, ear and eye,
Can be content with argument and
    deal
In abstract things ; or be derided by
A sort of battered kettle at the heel.

II

I pace upon the battlements and stare
On the foundations of a house, or
    where
Tree, like a sooty finger, starts from
    the earth ;
And send imagination forth
Under the day's declining beam, and
    call
Images and memories
From ruin or from ancient trees,
For I would ask a question of them all.

Beyond that ridge lived Mrs. French,
 and once
When every silver candlestick or
 sconce
Lit up the dark mahogany and the wine,
A serving man that could divine
That most respected lady's every wish,
Ran and with the garden shears
Clipped an insolent farmer's ears
And brought them in a little covered
 dish.

Some few remembered still when I was
 young
A peasant girl commended by a song,
Who'd lived somewhere upon that
 rocky place,
And praised the colour of her face,
And had the greater joy in praising
 her,
Remembering that, if walked she there,
Farmers jostled at the fair
So great a glory did the song confer.

And certain men, being maddened by
    those rhymes,
Or else by toasting her a score of times,
Rose from the table and declared it right
To test their fancy by their sight ;
But they mistook the brightness of
    the moon
For the prosaic light of day—
Music had driven their wits astray—
And one was drowned in the great bog
    of Cloone.

Strange, but the man who made the
    song was blind,
Yet, now I have considered it, I find
That nothing strange ; the tragedy
    began
With Homer that was a blind man,
And Helen has all living hearts
    betrayed.
O may the moon and sunlight seem
One inextricable beam,
For if I triumph I must make men mad.

And I myself created Hanrahan
And drove him drunk or sober through
    the dawn
From somewhere in the neighbouring
    cottages.
Caught by an old man's juggleries
He stumbled, tumbled, fumbled to and
    fro
And had but broken knees for hire
And horrible splendour of desire ;
I thought it all out twenty years ago :

Good fellows shuffled cards in an old
    bawn ;
And when that ancient ruffian's turn
    was on
He so bewitched the cards under his
    thumb
That all, but the one card, became
A pack of hounds and not a pack of
    cards,
And that he changed into a hare.
Hanrahan rose in frenzy there

And followed up those baying creatures
    towards—

O towards I have forgotten what—
    enough !
I must recall a man that neither love
Nor music nor an enemy's clipped ear
Could, he was so harried, cheer ;
A figure that has grown so fabulous
There's not a neighbour left to say
When he finished his dog's day :
An ancient bankrupt master of this
    house.

Before that ruin came, for centuries,
Rough men-at-arms, cross-gartered to
    the knees
Or shod in iron, climbed the narrow
    stairs,
And certain men-at-arms there were
Whose images, in the Great Memory
    stored,
Come with loud cry and panting breast

To break upon a sleeper's rest
While their great wooden dice beat on
    the board.

As I would question all, come all who
    can ;
Come old, necessitous, half-mounted
    man ;
And bring beauty's blind rambling
    celebrant ;
The red man the juggler sent
Through God-forsaken meadows ; Mrs.
    French,
Gifted with so fine an ear ;
The man drowned in a bog's mire,
When mocking muses chose the
    country wench.

Did all old men and women, rich and
    poor,
Who trod upon these rocks or passed
    this door,
Whether in public or in secret rage

As I do now against old age ?
But I have found an answer in those
  eyes
That are impatient to be gone ;
Go therefore ; but leave Hanrahan
For I need all his mighty memories.

Old lecher with a love on every wind
Bring up out of that deep considering
  mind
All that you have discovered in the
  grave,
For it is certain that you have
Reckoned up every unforeknown, un-
  seeing
Plunge, lured by a softening eye,
Or by a touch or a sigh,
Into the labyrinth of another's being ;

Does the imagination dwell the most
Upon a woman won or woman lost ?
If on the lost, admit you turned aside
From a great labyrinth out of pride,

Cowardice, some silly over-subtle
    thought
Or anything called conscience once;
And that if memory recur, the sun's
Under eclipse and the day blotted out.

III

It is time that I wrote my will;
I choose upstanding men,
That climb the streams until
The fountain leap, and at dawn
Drop their cast at the side
Of dripping stone; I declare
They shall inherit my pride,
The pride of people that were
Bound neither to Cause nor to State,
Neither to slaves that were spat on,
Nor to the tyrants that spat,
The people of Burke and of Grattan
That gave, though free to refuse—
Pride, like that of the morn,
When the headlong light is loose,
Or that of the fabulous horn,

Or that of the sudden shower
When all streams are dry,
Or that of the hour
When the swan must fix his eye
Upon a fading gleam,
Float out upon a long
Last reach of glittering stream
And there sing his last song.
And I declare my faith ;
I mock Plotinus' thought
And cry in Plato's teeth,
Death and life were not
Till man made up the whole,
Made lock, stock and barrel
Out of his bitter soul,
Aye, sun and moon and star, all,
And further add to that
That, being dead, we rise,
Dream and so create
Translunar Paradise.
I have prepared my peace
With learned Italian things
And the proud stones of Greece,

Poet's imaginings
And memories of love,
Memories of the words of women,
All those things whereof
Man makes a superhuman,
Mirror-resembling dream.

As at the loophole there,
The daws chatter and scream,
And drop twigs layer upon layer.
When they have mounted up,
The mother bird will rest
On their hollow top,
And so warm her wild nest.

I leave both faith and pride
To young upstanding men
Climbing the mountain side,
That under bursting dawn
They may drop a fly ;
Being of that metal made
Till it was broken by
This sedentary trade.

Now shall I make my soul
Compelling it to study
In a learned school
Till the wreck of body
Slow decay of blood,
Testy delirium
Or dull decrepitude,
Or what worse evil come—
The death of friends, or death
Of every brilliant eye
That made a catch in the breath—
Seem but the clouds of the sky
When the horizon fades ;
Or a bird's sleepy cry
Among the deepening shades.

1926

MEDITATIONS IN TIME OF CIVIL WAR

ANCESTRAL HOUSES

SURELY among a rich man's flowering
    lawns,
Amid the rustle of his planted hills,
Life overflows without ambitious
    pains ;
And rains down life until the basin
    spills,
And mounts more dizzy high the more
    it rains
As though to choose whatever shape
    it wills
And never stoop to a mechanical,
Or servile shape, at others' beck and
    call.

Mere dreams, mere dreams ! Yet
    Homer had not sung
Had he not found it certain beyond
    dreams
That out of life's own self-delight had
    sprung
The abounding glittering jet ; though
    now it seems
As if some marvellous empty sea-shell
    flung
Out of the obscure dark of the rich
    streams,
And not a fountain, were the symbol
    which
Shadows the inherited glory of the rich.

Some violent bitter man, some power-
    ful man
Called architect and artist in, that they,
Bitter and violent men, might rear in
    stone
The sweetness that all longed for night
    and day,

The gentleness none there had ever
   known ;
But when the master's buried mice
   can play,
And maybe the great-grandson of that
   house,
For all its bronze and marble, 's but a
   mouse.

Oh what if gardens where the peacock
   strays
With delicate feet upon old terraces,
Or else all Juno from an urn dis-
   plays
Before the indifferent garden deities ;
Oh what if levelled lawns and gravelled
   ways
Where slippered Contemplation finds
   his ease
And Childhood a delight for every
   sense,
But take our greatness with our
   violence !

What if the glory of escutcheoned
    doors,
And buildings that a haughtier age
    designed,
The pacing to and fro on polished
    floors
Amid great chambers and long
    galleries, lined
With famous portraits of our ancestors ;
What if those things the greatest of
    mankind,
Consider most to magnify, or to bless,
But take our greatness with our
    bitterness !

II

MY HOUSE

An ancient bridge, and a more ancient
    tower,
A farmhouse that is sheltered by its
    wall,

An acre of stony ground,
Where the symbolic rose can break in
    flower,
Old ragged elms, old thorns innumer-
    able,
The sound of the rain or sound
Of every wind that blows;
The stilted water-hen
Crossing stream again
Scared by the splashing of a dozen
    cows;

A winding stair, a chamber arched
    with stone,
A grey stone fireplace with an open
    hearth,
A candle and written page.
Il Penseroso's Platonist toiled on
In some like chamber, shadowing forth
How the daemonic rage
Imagined everything.
Benighted travellers
From markets and from fairs

Have seen his midnight candle glim-
    mering.

Two men have founded here. A man-
    at-arms
Gathered a score of horse and spent
    his days
In this tumultuous spot,
Where through long wars and sudden
    night alarms
His dwindling score and he seemed
    cast-a-ways
Forgetting and forgot ;
And I, that after me
My bodily heirs may find,
To exalt a lonely mind,
Befitting emblems of adversity.

III

MY TABLE

Two heavy tressels, and a board
Where Sato's gift, a changeless sword,

By pen and paper lies,
That it may moralise
My days out of their aimlessness.
A bit of an embroidered dress
Covers its wooden sheath.
Chaucer had not drawn breath
When it was forged.   In Sato's house,
Curved like new moon, moon luminous
It lay five hundred years.
Yet if no change appears
No moon ; only an aching heart
Conceives a changeless work of art.
Our learned men have urged
That when and where 'twas forged
A marvellous accomplishment,
In painting or in pottery, went
From father unto son
And through the centuries ran
And seemed   unchanging   like   the
      sword.
Soul's beauty being most adored,
Men and their business took
The soul's unchanging look ;

For the most rich inheritor,
Knowing that none could pass heaven's
    door
That loved inferior art,
Had such an aching heart
That he, although a country's talk
For silken clothes and stately walk,
Had waking wits ; it seemed
Juno's peacock screamed.

IV

MY DESCENDANTS

Having inherited a vigorous mind
From my old fathers I must nourish
    dreams
And leave a woman and a man behind
As vigorous of mind, and yet it seems
Life scarce can cast a fragrance on the
    wind,
Scarce spread a glory to the morning
    beams,

But the torn petals strew the garden
  plot ;
And there's but common greenness
  after that.

And what if my descendants lose the
  flower
Through natural declension of the soul,
Through too much business with the
  passing hour,
Through too much play, or marriage
  with a fool ?
May this laborious stair and this stark
  tower
Become a roofless ruin that the owl
May build in the cracked masonry
  and cry
Her desolation to the desolate sky.

The Primum Mobile that fashioned us
Has made the very owls in circles move;
And I, that count myself most
  prosperous,

Seeing that love and friendship are
    enough,
For an old neighbour's friendship
    chose the house
And decked and altered it for a girl's
    love,
And know whatever flourish and decline
These stones remain their monument
    and mine.

V

THE ROAD AT MY DOOR

An affable Irregular,
A heavily built Falstaffan man,
Comes cracking jokes of civil war
As though to die by gunshot were
The finest play under the sun.

A brown Lieutenant and his men,
Half dressed in national uniform,
Stand at my door, and I complain
Of the foul weather, hail and rain,
A pear tree broken by the storm.

I count those feathered balls of soot
The moor-hen guides upon the stream,
To silence the envy in my thought ;
And turn towards my chamber, caught
In the cold snows of a dream.

VI

THE STARE'S NEST BY MY WINDOW

The bees build in the crevices
Of loosening masonry, and there
The mother birds bring grubs and flies.
My wall is loosening ; honey-bees
Come build in the empty house of the
       stare.

We are closed in, and the key is turned
On our uncertainty ; somewhere
A man is killed, or a house burned,
Yet no clear fact to be discerned :
Come build in the empty house of the
       stare.

A barricade of stone or of wood ;
Some fourteen days of civil war ;
Last night they trundled down the road
That dead young soldier in his blood :
Come build in the empty house of the
    stare.

We had fed the heart on fantasies,
The heart's grown brutal from the fare,
More substance in our enmities
Than in our love ; oh, honey-bees
Come build in the empty house of the
    stare.

VII

I SEE PHANTOMS OF HATRED AND OF
    THE HEART'S FULLNESS AND OF
    THE COMING EMPTINESS

I climb to the tower top and lean upon
    broken stone,
A mist that is like blown snow is
    sweeping over all,

Valley, river, and elms, under the light
    of a moon
That seems unlike itself, that seems
    unchangeable,
A glittering sword out of the east. A
    puff of wind
And those white glimmering frag-
    ments of the mist sweep by.
Frenzies bewilder, reveries perturb
    the mind ;
Monstrous familiar images swim to
    the mind's eye.

' Vengeance upon the murderers,' the
    cry goes up,
' Vengeance for Jacques Molay.' In
    cloud-pale rags, or in lace,
The rage driven, rage tormented, and
    rage hungry troop,
Trooper belabouring trooper, biting at
    arm or at face,
Plunges towards nothing, arms and
    fingers spreading wide

For the embrace of nothing ; and I,
    my wits astray
Because of all that senseless tumult,
    all but cried
For vengeance on the murderers of
    Jacques Molay.

Their legs long delicate and slender,
    aquamarine their eyes,
Magical unicorns bear ladies on their
    backs,
The ladies close their musing eyes.
    No prophecies,
Remembered out of Babylonian
    almanacs,
Have closed the ladies' eyes, their
    minds are but a pool
Where even longing drowns under its
    own excess ;
Nothing but stillness can remain when
    hearts are full
Of their own sweetness, bodies of their
    loveliness.

The cloud-pale unicorns, the eyes of
    aquamarine,
The quivering half-closed eyelids, the
    rags of cloud or of lace,
Or eyes that rage has brightened, arms
    it has made lean,
Give place to an indifferent multitude,
    give place
To brazen hawks.   Nor self-delighting
    reverie,
Nor hate of what's to come, nor pity
    for what's gone,
Nothing but grip of claw, and the eye's
    complacency,
The innumerable clanging wings that
    have put out the moon.

I turn away and shut the door, and on
    the stair
Wonder how many times I could have
    proved my worth
In something that all others under-
    stand or share ;

But oh, ambitious heart had such a
    proof drawn forth
A company of friends, a conscience set
    at ease,
It had but made us pine the more.
    The abstract joy,
The half read wisdom of daemonic
    images,
Suffice the ageing man as once the
    growing boy.

1923

NINETEEN HUNDRED AND NINETEEN

I

MANY ingenious lovely things are gone
That seemed sheer miracle to the
multitude,
Protected from the circle of the moon
That pitches common things about.
There stood
Amid the ornamental bronze and stone
An ancient image made of olive wood—
And gone are Phidias' famous ivories
And all the golden grasshoppers and
bees.

We too had many pretty toys when
young ;
A law indifferent to blame or praise,

To bribe or threat ; habits that made
    old wrong
Melt down, as it were wax in the sun's
    rays ;
Public opinion ripening for so long
We thought it would outlive all future
    days.
O what fine thought we had because
    we thought
That the worst rogues and rascals had
    died out.

All teeth were drawn, all ancient
    tricks unlearned,
And a great army but a showy thing ;
What matter that no cannon had been
    turned
Into a ploughshare ; parliament and
    king
Thought that unless a little powder
    burned
The trumpeters might burst with
    trumpeting

D

And yet it lack all glory ; and per-
chance
The guardsmen's drowsy chargers would
not prance.

Now days are dragon - ridden, the
nightmare
Rides upon sleep : a drunken soldiery
Can leave the mother, murdered at
her door,
To crawl in her own blood, and go
scot-free ;
The night can sweat with terror as
before
We pieced our thoughts into philo-
sophy,
And planned to bring the world under
a rule,
Who are but weasels fighting in a
hole.

He who can read the signs nor sink
unmanned

Into the half-deceit of some intoxi-
    cant
From shallow wits ; who knows no
    work can stand,
Whether health, wealth or peace of
    mind were spent
On master work of intellect or hand,
No honour leave its mighty monument,
Has but one comfort left : all triumph
    would
But break upon his ghostly solitude.

But is there any comfort to be found ?
Man is in love and loves what vanishes,
What more is there to say ?   That
    country round
None dared admit, if such a thought
    were his,
Incendiary or bigot could be found
To burn that stump on the Acropolis,
Or break in bits the famous ivories
Or traffic in the grasshoppers or
    bees ?

II

When Loie Fuller's Chinese dancers
    enwound
A shining web, a floating ribbon of
    cloth,
It seemed that a dragon of air
Had fallen among dancers, had whirled
    them round
Or hurried them off on its own furious
    path ;
So the platonic year
Whirls out new right and wrong,
Whirls in the old instead ;
All men are dancers and their tread
Goes to the barbarous clangour of
    gong.

III

Some moralist or mythological poet
Compares the solitary soul to a swan ;
I am satisfied with that,

Satisfied if a troubled mirror show
    it
Before that brief gleam of its life be
    gone,
An image of its state ;
The wings half spread for flight,
The breast thrust out in pride
Whether to play, or to ride
Those winds that clamour of approach-
    ing night.

A man in his own secret meditation
Is lost amid the labyrinth that he has
    made
In art or politics ;
Some platonist affirms that in the
    station
Where we should cast off body and trade
The ancient habit sticks,
And that if our works could
But vanish with our breath
That were a lucky death,
For triumph can but mar our solitude.

The swan has leaped into the desolate
      heaven :
That image can bring wildness, bring
      a rage
To end all things, to end
What my laborious life imagined,
      even
The half imagined, the half written
      page ;
O but we dreamed to mend
Whatever mischief seemed
To afflict mankind, but now
That winds of winter blow
Learn that we were crack-pated when
      we dreamed.

IV

We, who seven years ago
Talked of honour and of truth,
Shriek with pleasure if we show
The weasel's twist, the weasel's tooth.

v

Come let us mock at the great
That had such burdens on the mind
And toiled so hard and late
To leave some monument behind,
Nor thought of the levelling wind.

Come let us mock at the wise ;
With all those calendars whereon
They fixed old aching eyes,
They never saw how seasons run,
And now but gape at the sun.

Come let us mock at the good
That fancied goodness might be gay,
And sick of solitude
Might proclaim a holiday :
Wind shrieked—and where are they ?

Mock mockers after that
That would not lift a hand maybe
To help good, wise or great

To bar that foul storm out, for we
Traffic in mockery.

VI

Violence upon the roads : violence of
    horses ;
Some few have handsome riders, are
    garlanded
On delicate sensitive ear or tossing
    mane,
But wearied running round and round
    in their courses
All break and vanish, and evil gathers
    head :
Herodias' daughters have returned
    again
A sudden blast of dusty wind and
    after
Thunder of feet, tumult of images,
Their purpose in the labyrinth of the
    wind ;

And should some crazy hand dare
    touch a daughter
All turn with amorous cries, or angry
    cries,
According to the wind, for all are blind.
But now wind drops, dust settles ;
    thereupon
There lurches past, his great eyes
    without thought
Under the shadow of stupid straw-
    pale locks,
That insolent fiend Robert Artisson
To whom the love-lorn Lady Kyteler
    brought
Bronzed peacock feathers, red combs
    of her cocks.

1919

THE WHEEL

THROUGH winter - time we call on
    spring,
And through the spring on summer call,
And when abounding hedges ring
Declare that winter's best of all ;
And after that there's nothing good
Because the spring - time has not
    come—
Nor know that what disturbs our
    blood
Is but its longing for the tomb.

YOUTH AND AGE

MUCH did I rage when young,
Being by the world oppressed,
But now with flattering tongue
It speeds the parting guest.

1924

THE NEW FACES

IF you, that have grown old, were the
    first dead,
Neither catalpa tree nor scented lime
Should hear my living feet, nor would
    I tread
Where we wrought that shall break
    the teeth of time.
Let the new faces play what tricks
    they will
In the old rooms; night can out-
    balance day,
Our shadows rove the garden gravel
    still,
The living seem more shadowy than
    they.

A PRAYER FOR MY SON

BID a strong ghost stand at the head
That my Michael may sleep sound,
Nor cry, nor turn in the bed
Till his morning meal come round ;
And may departing twilight keep
All dread afar till morning's back,
That his mother may not lack
Her fill of sleep.

Bid the ghost have sword in fist :
Some there are, for I avow
Such devilish things exist,
Who have planned his murder for
      they know
Of some most haughty deed or thought
That waits upon his future days,
And would through hatred of the bays
Bring that to nought.

Though You can fashion everything
From nothing every day, and teach
The morning stars to sing,
You have lacked articulate speech
To tell Your simplest want, and known,
Wailing upon a woman's knee,
All of that worst ignominy
Of flesh and bone ;

And when through all the town there
    ran
The servants of Your enemy,
A woman and a man,
Unless the Holy Writings lie,
Hurried through the smooth and rough
And through the fertile and waste,
Protecting, till the danger past,
With human love.

TWO SONGS FROM A PLAY

I saw a staring virgin stand
Where holy Dionysus died,
And tear the heart out of his side,
And lay the heart upon her hand
And bear that beating heart away ;
And then did all the Muses sing
Of Magnus Annus at the spring,
As though God's death were but a play.

Another Troy must rise and set,
Another lineage feed the crow,
Another Argo's painted prow
Drive to a flashier bauble yet.
The Roman Empire stood appalled :
It dropped the reins of peace and war
When that fierce virgin and her Star
Out of the fabulous darkness called.

That cognomen sounded best
Considering what wild infancy
Drove horror from His Mother's
    breast.

LEDA AND THE SWAN

A SUDDEN blow : the great wings
    beating still
Above the staggering girl, her thighs
    caressed
By the dark webs, her nape caught in
    his bill,
He holds her helpless breast upon his
    breast.

How can those terrified vague fingers
    push
The feathered glory from her loosening
    thighs ?
And how can body, laid in that white
    rush
But feel the strange heart beating
    where it lies ?

51

A shudder in the loins engenders there
The broken wall, the burning roof and
  tower
And Agamemnon dead.
                    Being so caught up,
So mastered by the brute blood of the
  air,
Did she put on his knowledge with his
  power
Before the indifferent beak could let
  her drop ?

1923

ON A PICTURE OF A BLACK
CENTAUR BY EDMOND DULAC

YOUR hooves have stamped at the
    black margin of the wood,
Even where horrible green parrots call
    and swing.
My works are all stamped down into
    the sultry mud.
I knew that horse play, knew it for a
    murderous thing.
What wholesome sun has ripened is
    wholesome food to eat
And that alone; yet I, being driven
    half insane
Because of some green wing, gathered
    old mummy wheat
In the mad abstract dark and ground
    it grain by grain

And after baked it slowly in an oven ;
    but now
I bring full flavoured wine out of a
    barrel found
Where seven Ephesian topers slept
    and never knew
When Alexander's empire past, they
    slept so sound.
Stretch out your limbs and sleep a
    long Saturnian sleep ;
I have loved you better than my soul
    for all my words,
And there is none so fit to keep a
    watch and keep
Unwearied eyes upon those horrible
    green birds.

AMONG SCHOOL CHILDREN

I

I WALK through the long schoolroom
    questioning,
A kind old nun in a white hood replies ;
The children learn to cipher and to
    sing,
To study reading-books and history,
To cut and sew, be neat in everything
In the best modern way—the chil-
    dren's eyes
In momentary wonder stare upon
A sixty year old smiling public man.

II

I dream of a Ledæan body, bent
Above a sinking fire, a tale that she

Told of a harsh reproof, or trivial event
That changed some childish day to
      tragedy—
Told, and it seemed that our two
      natures blent
Into a sphere from youthful sympathy,
Or else, to alter Plato's parable,
Into the yolk and white of the one
      shell.

III

And thinking of that fit of grief or
      rage
I look upon one child or t'other there
And wonder if she stood so at that
      age—
For even daughters of the swan can
      share
Something of every paddler's heri-
      tage—
And had that colour upon cheek or
      hair

And thereupon my heart is driven wild :
She stands before me as a living child.

IV

Her present image floats in to the
    mind—
Did quattrocento finger fashion it
Hollow of cheek as though it drank
    the wind
And took a mass of shadows for its
    meat ?
And I though never of Ledæan kind
Had pretty plumage once—enough of
    that,
Better to smile on all that smile, and
    show
There is a comfortable kind of old
    scarecrow.

V

What youthful mother, a shape upon
    her lap

Honey of generation had betrayed,
And that must sleep, shriek, struggle
    to escape
As recollection or the drug decide,
Would think her son, did she but see
    that shape
With sixty or more winters on its
    head,
A compensation for the pang of his
    birth,
Or the uncertainty of his setting
    forth ?

VI

Plato thought nature but a spume
    that plays
Upon a ghostly paradigm of things ;
Solider Aristotle played the taws
Upon the bottom of a king of kings ;
World-famous golden-thighed Pytha-
    goras
Fingered upon a fiddle stick or strings

What a star sang and careless Muses
    heard :
Old clothes upon old sticks to scare
    a bird.

VII

Both nuns and mothers worship images,
But those the candles light are not as
    those
That animate a mother's reveries,
But keep a marble or a bronze repose.
And yet they too break hearts — O
    Presences
That passion, piety or affection knows,
And that all heavenly glory sym-
    bolise—
O self-born mockers of man's enter-
    prise ;

VIII

Labour is blossoming or dancing where
The body is not bruised to pleasure soul,

Nor beauty born out of its own
    despair,
Nor blear-eyed wisdom out of midnight
    oil.
O chestnut tree, great rooted blossomer,
Are you the leaf, the blossom or the
    bole ?
O body swayed to music, O brighten-
    ing glance,
How can we know the dancer from the
    dance ?

COLONUS' PRAISE

(From 'Oedipus at Colonus')

CHORUS

COME praise Colonus' horses and come
    praise
The wine dark of the wood's intri-
    cacies,
The nightingale that deafens daylight
    there,
If daylight ever visit where,
Unvisited by tempest or by sun,
Immortal ladies tread the ground
Dizzy with harmonious sound,
Semele's lad a gay companion.

And yonder in the gymnasts' garden
    thrives

The self-sown, self-begotten shape that
    gives
Athenian intellect its mastery,
Even the grey-leaved olive tree
Miracle-bred out of the living stone ;
Nor accident of peace nor war
Shall wither that old marvel, for
The great grey - eyed Athene stares
    thereon.

Who comes into this country, and has
    come
Where golden crocus and narcissus
    bloom,
Where the Great Mother, mourning
    for her daughter
And beauty-drunken by the water
Glittering among grey - leaved olive
    trees,
Has plucked a flower and sung her loss ;
Who finds abounding Cephisus
Has found the loveliest spectacle there
    is.

Because this country has a pious mind
And so remembers that when all
    mankind
But trod the road, or paddled by the
    shore,
Poseidon gave it bit and oar,
Every Colonus lad or lass discourses
Of that oar and of that bit ;
Summer and winter, day and night,
Of horses and horses of the sea, white
    horses.

THE HERO, THE GIRL, AND
THE FOOL

THE GIRL

I RAGE at my own image in the glass,
That's so unlike myself that when you
    praise it
It is as though you praised another,
    or even
Mocked me with praise of my mere
    opposite;
And when I wake towards morn I
    dread myself
For the heart cries that what deception
    wins
Cruelty must keep; therefore be
    warned and go
If you have seen that image and not
    the woman.

The Hero

I have raged at my own strength
    because you have loved it.

The Girl

If you are no more strength than I am
    beauty
I had better find a convent and turn
    nun ;
A nun at least has all men's rever-
    ence
And needs no cruelty.

The Hero

        I have heard one say
That men have reverence for their
    holiness
And not themselves.

                F

THE GIRL

              Say on and say
That only God has loved us for ourselves,
But what care I that long for a man's
    love ?

THE FOOL BY THE ROADSIDE

When my days that have
From cradle run to grave
From grave to cradle run instead ;
When thoughts that a fool
Has wound upon a spool
Are but loose thread, are but loose
    thread.

When cradle and spool are past
And I mere shade at last
Coagulate of stuff
Transparent like the wind,
I think that I may find
A faithful love, a faithful love.

OWEN AHERN AND HIS
DANCERS

I

A STRANGE thing surely that my heart
    when love had come unsought
Upon the Norman upland or in that
    poplar shade,
Should find no burden but itself and
    yet should be worn out.
It could not bear that burden and
    therefore it went mad.

The south wind brought it longing, and
    the east wind despair,
The west wind made it pitiful, and the
    north wind afraid.
It feared to give its love a hurt with all
    the tempest there ;

It feared the hurt that she could give
    and therefore it went mad.

I can exchange opinion with any
    neighbouring mind,
I have as healthy flesh and blood as
    any rhymer's had,
But oh my Heart could bear no more
    when the upland caught the wind;
I ran, I ran, from my love's side
    because my Heart went mad.

II

The Heart behind its rib laughed out,
    'You have called me mad,' it said.
'Because I made you turn away and
    run from that young child;
How could she mate with fifty years
    that was so wildly bred?
Let the cage bird and the cage bird
    mate and the wild bird mate in
    the wild.'

'You but imagine lies all day, O
    murderer,' I replied.
'And all those lies have but one end
    poor wretches to betray ;
I did not find in any cage the woman
    at my side.
O but her heart would break to learn
    my thoughts are far away.'

'Speak all your mind,' my Heart sang
    out, 'speak all your mind ; who
    cares,
Now that your tongue cannot persuade
    the child till she mistake
Her childish gratitude for love and
    match your fifty years.
O let her choose a young man now and
    all for his wild sake.'

A MAN YOUNG AND OLD

THOUGH nurtured like the sailing moon
In beauty's murderous brood,
She walked awhile and blushed awhile
And on my pathway stood
Until I thought her body bore
A heart of flesh and blood.

But since I laid a hand thereon
And found a heart of stone
I have attempted many things
And not a thing is done,
For every hand is lunatic
That travels on the moon.

She smiled and that transfigured me
And left me but a lout,

Maundering   here,   and   maundering
    there,
Emptier of thought
Than heavenly circuit of its stars
When the moon sails out.

HUMAN DIGNITY

Like the moon her kindness is,
If kindness I may call
What has no comprehension in't,
But is the same for all
As though my sorrow were a scene
Upon a painted wall.

So like a bit of stone I lie
Under a broken tree.
I could recover if I shrieked
My heart's agony
To passing bird, but I am dumb
From human dignity.

THE MERMAID

A mermaid found a swimming lad,
Picked him for her own,
Pressed her body to his body,
Laughed ; and plunging down
Forgot in cruel happiness
That even lovers drown.

THE DEATH OF THE HARE

I have pointed out the yelling pack,
The hare leap to the wood,
And when I pass a compliment
Rejoice as lover should
At the drooping of an eye
At the mantling of the blood.

Then suddenly my heart is wrung
By her distracted air
And I remember wildness lost
And after, swept from there,
Am set down standing in the wood
At the death of the hare.

THE EMPTY CUP

A crazy man that found a cup,
When all but dead of thirst,
Hardly dared to wet his mouth
Imagining, moon accursed,
That another mouthful
And his beating heart would burst.
October last I found it too
But found it dry as bone,
And for that reason am I crazed
And my sleep is gone.

HIS MEMORIES

We should be hidden from their
    eyes,
Being but holy shows
And bodies broken like a thorn
Whereon the bleak north blows,
To think of buried Hector
And that none living knows.

The women take so little stock
In what I do or say
They'd sooner leave their cosseting
To hear a jackass bray;
My arms are like the twisted thorn
And yet there beauty lay;

The first of all the tribe lay there
And did such pleasure take—
She who had brought great Hector
    down
And put all Troy to wreck—
That she cried into this ear
Strike me if I shriek.

THE FRIENDS OF HIS YOUTH

Laughter not time destroyed my
    voice
And put that crack in it,
And when the moon's pot-bellied
I get a laughing fit,

For that old Madge comes down the lane
A stone upon her breast,
And a cloak wrapped about the stone,
And she can get no rest
With singing hush and hush-a-bye ;
She that has been wild
And barren as a breaking wave
Thinks that the stone's a child.
And Peter that had great affairs
And was a pushing man
Shrieks ' I am King of the Peacocks,'
And perches on a stone ;
And then I laugh till tears run down
And the heart thumps at my side,
Remembering that her shriek was love
And that he shrieks from pride.

SUMMER AND SPRING

We sat under an old thorn-tree
And talked away the night,
Told all that had been said or done
Since first we saw the light,

And when we talked of growing up
Knew that we'd halved a soul
And fell the one in t'other's arms
That we might make it whole ;
Then Peter had a murdering look
For it seemed that he and she
Had spoken of their childish days
Under that very tree.
O what a bursting out there was,
And what a blossoming,
When we had all the summer time
And she had all the spring.

THE SECRETS OF THE OLD

I have old women's secrets now
That had those of the young ;
Madge tells me what I dared not
    think
When my blood was strong,
And what had drowned a lover once
Sounds like an old song.

Though Margery is stricken dumb
If thrown in Madge's way,
We three make up a solitude;
For none alive to-day
Can know the stories that we know
Or say the things we say:

How such a man pleased women
   most
Of all that are gone,
How such a pair loved many years
And such a pair but one,
Stories of the bed of straw
Or the bed of down.

HIS WILDNESS

O bid me mount and sail up there
Amid the cloudy wrack,
For Peg and Meg and Paris' love
That had so straight a back,
Are gone away, and some that stay,
Have changed their silk for sack.

Were I but there and none to hear
I'd have a peacock cry
For that is natural to a man
That lives in memory,
Being all alone I'd nurse a stone
And sing it lullaby.

THE THREE MONUMENTS

THEY hold their public meetings where
Our most renowned patriots stand,
One among the birds of the air,
A stumpier on either hand ;
And all the popular statesmen say
That purity built up the state
And after kept it from decay ;
Admonish us to cling to that
And let all base ambition be,
For intellect would make us proud
And pride bring in impurity :
The three old rascals laugh aloud.

FROM 'OEDIPUS AT COLONUS'

I

ENDURE what life God gives and ask no
    longer span ;
Cease to remember the delights of
    youth, travel-wearied aged man ;
Delight becomes death-longing if all
    longing else be vain.

II

Even from that delight memory
    treasures so,
Death, despair, division of families,
    all entanglements of mankind
    grow,
As that old wandering beggar and
    these God-hated children know.

III

In the long echoing street the laughing
    dancers throng,
The bride is carried to the bridegroom's
    chamber through torchlight and
    tumultuous song;
I celebrate the silent kiss that ends
    short life or long.

IV

Never to have lived is best, ancient
    writers say ;
Never to have drawn the breath of life,
    never to have looked into the eye
    of day;
The second best's a gay goodnight and
    quickly turn away.

THE GIFT OF HARUN
AL-RASHID

KUSTA BEN LUKA is my name, I write
To Abd Al-Rabban ; fellow roysterer
    once,
Now the good Caliph's learned
    Treasurer,
And for no ear but his.

               Carry this letter
Through the great gallery of the
    Treasure House
Where banners of the Caliphs hang,
    night-coloured
But brilliant as the night's embroidery,
And wait war's music ; pass the little
    gallery ;
Pass books of learning from Byzantium
Written in gold upon a purple stain,

And pause at last, I was about to say,
At the great book of Sappho's song;
    but no,
For should you leave my letter there,
    a boy's
Love - lorn, indifferent hands might
    come upon it
And let it fall unnoticed to the floor.
Pause at the Treatise of Parmenides
And hide it there, for Caliphs to
    world's end
Must keep that perfect, as they keep
    her song
So great its fame.
        When fitting time has passed
The parchment will disclose to some
    learned man
A mystery that else had found no
    chronicler
But the wild Bedouin. Though I
    approve
Those wanderers that welcomed in
    their tents

What great Harun Al-Rashid, occupied
With Persian embassy or Grecian
    war,
Must needs neglect ; I cannot hide
    the truth
That wandering in a desert, featureless
As air under a wing, can give birds'
    wit.
In after time they will speak much of
    me
And speak but phantasy. Recall the
    year
When our beloved Caliph put to death
His Vizir Jaffer for an unknown
    reason ;
'If but the shirt upon my body
    knew it
I'd tear it off and throw it in the
    fire.'
That speech was all that the town
    knew, but he
Seemed for a while to have grown
    young again ;

Seemed so on purpose, muttered
    Jaffer's friends,
That none might know that he was
    conscience struck—
But that's a traitor's thought.
    Enough for me
That in the early summer of the year
The mightiest of the princes of the
    world
Came to the least considered of his
    courtiers ;
Sat down upon the fountain's marble
    edge
One hand amid the goldfish in the
    pool ;
And thereupon a colloquy took place
That I commend to all the chroniclers
To show how violent great hearts can
    lose
Their bitterness and find the honey-
    comb.
' I have brought a slender bride into
    the house ;

You know the saying " Change the
    bride with Spring ",
And she and I, being sunk in happi-
    ness,
Cannot endure to think you tread
    these paths,
When evening stirs the jasmine, and yet
Are brideless.'
                ' I am falling into years.'

' But such as you and I do not seem old
Like men who live by habit. Every
    day
I ride with falcon to the river's edge
Or carry the ringed mail upon my back,
Or court a woman ; neither enemy,
Game-bird, nor woman does the same
    thing twice ;
And so a hunter carries in the eye
A mimicry of youth. Can poet's
    thought
That springs from body and in body
    falls

Like this pure jet, now lost amid blue
    sky
Now bathing lily leaf and fishes' scale,
Be mimicry ? '
          ' What matter if our souls
Are nearer to the surface of the body
Than souls that start no game and
    turn no rhyme !
The soul's own youth and not the
    body's youth
Shows through our lineaments. My
    candle's bright,
My lantern is too loyal not to show
That it was made in your great
    father's reign.'

' And yet the jasmine season warms
    our blood.'

' Great prince, forgive the freedom of
    my speech ;
You think that love has seasons, and
    you think

That if the spring bear off what the
    spring gave
The heart need suffer no defeat; but I
Who have accepted the Byzantine
    faith,
That seems unnatural to Arabian
    minds,
Think when I choose a bride I choose
    for ever;
And if her eye should not grow bright
    for mine
Or brighten only for some younger eye,
My heart could never turn from daily
    ruin,
Nor find a remedy.'

                               ' But what if I
Have lit upon a woman, who so shares
Your thirst for those old crabbed
    mysteries,
So strains to look beyond our life, an
    eye
That never knew that strain would
    scarce seem bright,

And yet herself can seem youth's very
    fountain,
Being all brimmed with life.'
                     ' Were it but true
I would have found the best that life
    can give,
Companionship in those mysterious
    things
That make a man's soul or a woman's
    soul
Itself and not some other soul.'
                      ' That love
Must needs be in this life and in what
    follows
Unchanging and at peace, and it is right
Every philosopher should praise that
    love.
But I being none can praise its
    opposite.
It makes my passion stronger but to
    think
Like passion stirs the peacock and his
    mate,

The wild stag and the doe; that
    mouth to mouth
Is a man's mockery of the changeless
    soul.'
And thereupon his bounty gave what
    now
Can shake more blossom from autumnal
    chill
Than all my bursting springtime knew.
    A girl
Perched in some window of her
    mother's house
Had watched my daily passage to and
    fro;
Had heard impossible history of my
    past;
Imagined some impossible history
Lived at my side; thought time's
    disfiguring touch
Gave but more reason for a woman's
    care.
Yet was it love of me, or was it
    love

Of the stark mystery that has dazed
 my sight,
Perplexed her phantasy and planned
 her care ?
Or did the torchlight of that mystery
Pick out my features in such light and
 shade
Two contemplating passions chose one
 theme
Through sheer bewilderment ? She
 had not paced
The garden paths, nor counted up the
 rooms,
Before she had spread a book upon
 her knees
And asked about the pictures or the
 text ;
And often those first days I saw her
 stare
On old dry writing in a learned
 tongue,
On old dry faggots that could never
 please

The extravagance of spring ; or move
    a hand
As if that writing or the figured page
Were some dear cheek.
              Upon a moonless night
I sat where I could watch her sleeping
    form,
And wrote by candle - light ; but her
    form moved,
And fearing that my light disturbed
    her sleep
I rose that I might screen it with a
    cloth.
I heard her voice, ' Turn that I may
    expound
What's bowed your shoulder and made
    pale your cheek ' ;
And saw her sitting upright on the
    bed ;
Or was it she that spoke or some great
    Djinn ?
I say that a Djinn spoke.   A live-long
    hour

She seemed the learned man and I the
    child ;
Truths without father came, truths
    that no book
Of all the uncounted books that I have
    read,
Nor thought out of her mind or mine
    begot,
Self - born, high - born, and solitary
    truths,
Those terrible implacable straight lines
Drawn through the wandering vege-
    tative dream,
Even those truths that when my bones
    are dust
Must drive the Arabian host.
                 The voice grew still,
And she lay down upon her bed and slept,
But woke at the first gleam of day,
    rose up
And swept the house and sang about
    her work
In childish ignorance of all that passed.

A dozen nights of natural sleep, and
    then
When the full moon swam to its
    greatest height
She rose, and with her eyes shut fast
    in sleep
Walked through the house. Un-
    noticed and unfelt
I wrapped her in a heavy hooded
    cloak, and she,
Half running, dropped at the first
    ridge of the desert
And there marked out those emblems
    on the sand
That day by day I study and marvel at,
With her white finger.　I led her home
    asleep
And once again she rose and swept the
    house
In childish ignorance of all that passed.
Even to-day, after some seven years
When maybe thrice in every moon her
    mouth

Murmured the wisdom of the desert
    Djinns,
She keeps that ignorance, nor has
    she now
That first unnatural interest in my
    books.
It seems enough that I am there ;
    and yet
Old fellow student, whose most patient
    ear
Heard all the anxiety of my passionate
    youth,
It seems I must buy knowledge with
    my peace.
What if she lose her ignorance and so
Dream that I love her only for the
    voice,
That every gift and every word of
    praise
Is but a payment for that midnight
    voice
That is to age what milk is to a
    child !

Were she to lose her love, because she
    had lost
Her confidence in mine, or even lose
Its first simplicity, love, voice and all,
All my fine feathers would be plucked
    away
And I left shivering. The voice has
    drawn
A quality of wisdom from her love's
Particular quality. The signs and
    shapes ;
All those abstractions that you fancied
    were
From the great treatise of Parmenides ;
All, all those gyres and cubes and
    midnight things
Are but a new expression of her body
Drunk with the bitter sweetness of her
    youth.
And now my utmost mystery is out.
A woman's beauty is a storm-tossed
    banner ;
Under it wisdom stands, and I alone—

Of all Arabia's lovers I alone—
Nor dazzled by the embroidery, nor
    lost
In the confusion of its night - dark
    folds,
Can hear the armed man speak.

1923

ALL SOULS' NIGHT

AN EPILOGUE TO 'A VISION'

MIDNIGHT has come and the great
    Christ Church Bell,
And many a lesser bell, sound through
    the room ;
And it is All Souls' Night,
And two long glasses brimmed with
    muscatel
Bubble upon the table.   A ghost may
    come ;
For it is a ghost's right,
His element is so fine
Being sharpened by his death,
To drink from the wine-breath
While our gross palates drink from
    the whole wine.

I need some mind that, if the cannon
    sound
From every quarter of the world, can
    stay
Wound in mind's pondering,
As mummies in the mummy-cloth are
    wound ;
Because I have a marvellous thing to
    say,
A certain marvellous thing
None but the living mock,
Though not for sober ear ;
It may be all that hear
Should laugh and weep an hour upon
    the clock.

H—'s the first I call. He loved
    strange thought
And knew that sweet extremity of
    pride
That's called platonic love,
And that to such a pitch of passion
    wrought

Nothing could bring him, when his
    lady died,
Anodyne for his love.
Words were but wasted breath ;
One dear hope had he :
The inclemency
Of that or the next winter would be
    death.

Two thoughts were so mixed up I
    could not tell
Whether of her or God he thought the
    most,
But think that his mind's eye,
When upward turned, on one sole
    image fell ;
And that a slight companionable ghost,
Wild with divinity,
Had so lit up the whole
Immense miraculous house,
The Bible promised us,
It seemed a gold-fish swimming in a
    bowl.

On Florence Emery I call the next,
Who finding the first wrinkles on a face
Admired and beautiful,
And knowing that the future would
      be vexed
With 'minished beauty, multiplied
      commonplace,
Preferred to teach a school,
Away from neighbour or friend
Among dark skins, and there
Permit foul years to wear
Hidden from eyesight to the un-
      noticed end.

Before that end much had she ravelled
      out
From a discourse in figurative speech
By some learned Indian
On the soul's journey. How it is
      whirled about,
Wherever the orbit of the moon can
      reach,
Until it plunge into the sun ;

And there, free and yet fast
Being both Chance and Choice,
Forget its broken toys
And sink into its own delight at last.

And I call up MacGregor from the
    grave,
For in my first hard springtime we
    were friends,
Although of late estranged.
I thought him half a lunatic, half
    knave,
And told him so, but friendship never
    ends ;
And what if mind seem changed,
And it seem changed with the mind,
When thoughts rise up unbid
On generous things that he did
And I grow half contented to be blind.

He had much industry at setting out,
Much boisterous courage, before loneli-
    ness

Had driven him crazed ;
For   meditations   upon   unknown
    thought
Make human intercourse grow less and
    less ;
They are neither paid nor praised.
But he'd object to the host,
The glass because my glass ;
A ghost-lover he was
And may have grown more arrogant
    being a ghost.

But names are nothing.   What matter
    who it be,
So that his elements have grown so
    fine
The fume of muscatel
Can give his sharpened palate ecstasy
No living man can drink from the
    whole wine.
I have mummy truths to tell
Whereat the living mock,
Though not for sober ear,

For maybe all that hear
Should laugh and weep an hour upon
  the clock.

Such thought — such thought have I
  that hold it tight
Till meditation master all its parts,
Nothing can stay my glance
Until that glance run in the world's
  despite
To where the damned have howled
  away their hearts,
And where the blessed dance ;
Such thought, that in it bound
I need no other thing
Wound in mind's wandering,
As mummies in the mummy-cloth are
  wound.

NOTES

SAILING TO BYZANTIUM
Stanza IV

I have read somewhere that in the Emperor's palace at Byzantium was a tree made of gold and silver, and artificial birds that sang.

THE TOWER. Part II

The persons mentioned are associated by legend, story and tradition with the neighbourhood of Thoor Ballylee or Ballylee Castle, where the poem was written.   Mrs. French lived at Peterswell in the eighteenth century and was related to Sir Jonah Barrington, who described the incident of the ear and the trouble that came of it.   The peasant beauty and the blind poet are Mary Hynes and Raftery, and the incident of the man drowned in Cloone Bog is recorded in my *Celtic Twilight*.   Hanrahan's

pursuit of the phantom hare and hounds is from my *Stories of Red Hanrahan*. The ghosts have been seen at their game of dice in what is now my bedroom, and the old bankrupt man lived about a hundred years ago. According to one legend he could only leave the Castle upon a Sunday because of his creditors, and according to another he hid in the secret passage.

THE TOWER. PART III

In the passage about the Swan I have unconsciously echoed one of the loveliest lyrics of our time—Mr. Sturge Moore's 'Dying Swan'. I often recited it during an American lecturing tour, which explains the theft.

THE DYING SWAN

O silver-throated Swan
Struck, struck ! A golden dart
Clean through thy breast has gone
Home to thy heart.
Thrill, thrill, O silver throat !
O silver trumpet, pour
Love for defiance back

On him who smote !
And brim, brim o'er
With love ; and ruby-dye thy track
Down thy last living reach
Of river, sail the golden light—
Enter the sun's heart—even teach,
O wondrous-gifted pain, teach thou
The God to love, let him learn how !

When I wrote the lines about Plato and
Plotinus I forgot that it is something in our
own eyes that makes us see them as all tran-
scendence. Has not Plotinus written : ' Let
every soul recall, then, at the outset the truth
that soul is the author of all living things, that
it has breathed the life into them all, whatever
is nourished by earth and sea, all the creatures
of the air, the divine stars in the sky ; it is the
maker of the sun ; itself formed and ordered
this vast heaven and conducts all that rhythmic
motion — and it is a principle distinct from
all these to which it gives law and movement
and life, and it must of necessity be more
honourable than they, for they gather or
dissolve as soul brings them life or abandons
them, but soul, since it never can abandon
itself, is of eternal being '.

MEDITATIONS IN TIME OF
CIVIL WAR

These poems were written at Thoor Ballylee in 1922, during the civil war. Before they were finished the Republicans blew up our ' ancient bridge ' one midnight. They forbade us to leave the house, but were otherwise polite, even saying at last ' Goodnight, thank you ' as though we had given them the bridge.

SECTION SIX

In the West of Ireland we call a starling a stare, and during the civil war one built in a hole in the masonry by my bedroom window.

SECTION SEVEN, STANZA II

The cry ' Vengeance on the murderers of Jacques Molay ', Grand Master of the Templars, seems to me fit symbol for those who labour from hatred, and so for sterility in various kinds. It is said to have been incorporated in the ritual of certain Masonic societies of the eighteenth century, and to have fed class-hatred.

SECTION SEVEN, STANZA IV

I have a ring with a hawk and a butterfly upon it, to symbolise the straight road of logic, and so of mechanism, and the crooked road of intuition : ' For wisdom is a butterfly and not a gloomy bird of prey '.

NINETEEN HUNDRED AND NINETEEN
SECTION SIX

The country people see at times certain apparitions whom they name now ' fallen angels ', now ' ancient inhabitants of the country ', and describe as riding at whiles ' with flowers upon the heads of the horses '. I have assumed in the sixth poem that these horsemen, now that the times worsen, give way to worse. My last symbol, Robert Artisson, was an evil spirit much run after in Kilkenny at the start of the fourteenth century. Are not those who travel in the whirling dust also in the Platonic Year ?

TWO SONGS FROM A PLAY

These songs are sung by the Chorus in a play that has for its theme Christ's first appearance

to the Apostles after the Resurrection, a play
intended for performance in a drawing-room
or studio.

AMONG SCHOOL CHILDREN
Stanza III

I have taken ' the honey of generation '
from Porphyry's essay on ' The Cave of the
Nymphs ', but find no warrant in Porphyry
for considering it the ' drug ' that destroys
the ' recollection ' of pre-natal freedom.   He
blamed a cup of oblivion given in the zodiacal
sign of Cancer.

THE GIFT OF HARUN AL-RASHID

Part of an unfinished set of poems, dialogues
and stories about John Ahern and Michael
Robartes, Kusta ben Luka, a philosopher of
Bagdad, and his Bedouin followers.

THE END

Printed in Great Britain by R. & R. CLARK, LIMITED, *Edinburgh.*

BY W. B. YEATS

RESPONSIBILITIES AND OTHER POEMS. Crown
8vo. 4s. 6d. net.

THE WILD SWANS AT COOLE. Poems. Crown 8vo.
3s. 6d. net.

THE TOWER. Crown 8vo. 6s. net.

SOPHOCLES' KING OEDIPUS. A Version for the
Modern Stage. Crown 8vo. 2s. 6d. net.

SOPHOCLES' OEDIPUS AT COLONUS. Crown 8vo.
2s. 6d. net.

FOUR PLAYS FOR DANCERS. Illustrated by
EDMUND DULAC. Fcap 4to. 5s. net.

THE PLAYER QUEEN. Globe 8vo. 1s. net.

THE CUTTING OF AN AGATE. Essays. Crown 8vo.
4s. 6d. net.

REVERIES OVER CHILDHOOD AND YOUTH.
Illustrated. Crown 8vo. 4s. 6d. net.

MACMILLAN AND CO., LTD., LONDON.

2

NOTES TO YEATS'S NOTES
TO *THE TOWER*

SAILING TO BYZANTIUM—STANZA IV

The emperor was Theophilus, who ruled from 829 until his death in 842; "somewhere" is most likely *The History of the Decline and Fall of the Roman Empire* (1776–88) by the English historian Edward Gibbon (1737–94).

THE TOWER—PART II

In March 1917 Yeats purchased "Ballylee Castle," a Norman tower constructed in the thirteenth or fourteenth century, with two attached cottages. He restored the property and lived there for several summers, naming it Thoor Ballylee, "Thoor" being his rendition of the Irish *túr,* tower.

The story of Mrs. French is found in the chapter on "Irish Gentry and Their Retainers" in *Personal Sketches of His Own Times* (1827–32) by Sir Jonah Barrington (1760–1834). The event occurred in 1778.

Mary Hynes was a celebrated beauty who died in the 1840s. The blind Irish poet Anthony Raftery (Antoine Raiftearaí, 1779–1835) wrote of her in "Mary Hynes, or The Posy Bright" in *Songs Ascribed to Raftery,* ed. Douglas Hyde (1903). Yeats wrote of her in "'Dust Hath Closed Helen's Eye,'" a story added to the 1902 edition of *The Celtic Twilight* and which included a translation by Lady Gregory of Raftery's poem.

Hanrahan is an invented character, largely based on the

Gaelic poet Owen Roe O'Sullivan (Eoghan Rua Ó Súilleabhán, 1748–84). Yeats refers to his *Stories of Red Hanrahan* (1905).

THE TOWER—Part III

"The Dying Swan" by T. Sturge Moore (1870–1944), an English writer and artist and friend of Yeats (and the designer of the book cover of *The Tower*), was first published in *The Sea Is Kind* (1914). Yeats lectured in America from January to May 1920.

Plato (ca. 429–ca. 347 B.C.), Greek philosopher; Plotinus (205–269/70), Roman Neoplatonic philosopher, possibly born in Egypt. Yeats quotes from *Plotinus: The Divine Mind, Being the Treatises of the Fifth Ennead,* trans. Stephen MacKenna (1926).

MEDITATIONS IN TIME OF CIVIL WAR

The Irish Civil War was fought in 1922–23 between the Free State Government and the Republicans, the latter not accepting the terms of the Anglo-Irish Treaty, signed in London on 6 December 1921 and approved by the Irish parliament on 7 January 1922.

MEDITATIONS IN TIME OF CIVIL WAR— SECTION SEVEN, STANZA II

The Knights Templar were formed in 1118 as a monastic-military order to defend the Christian realm and to protect pilgrims visiting the Holy Land; the order was dissolved by Pope Clement V in 1312. Jacques de Molay (1244–1314) was burned at the stake after repudiating his recantation. Freemason societies, which began in the seventeenth century, were often considered as anti-Catholic associations.

MEDITATIONS IN TIME OF CIVIL WAR—
SECTION SEVEN, STANZA IV

Yeats's ring was designed by his friend the English artist Edmund Dulac (1882–1953). Yeats slightly misquotes "Tom O'Roughley," first published in *The Little Review* (October 1918) and included in *The Wild Swans at Coole* (1919).

NINETEEN HUNDRED AND NINETEEN—
SECTION SIX

Yeats discusses the alternative explanations in his note on "The Trooping Fairies" in *Fairy and Folk Tales of the Irish Peasantry* (1888). The detail of the flowers is included in his essay "The Tribes of Danu" in *The New Review* (November 1897).

Robert Artisson appears in *The Historie of Ireland* (1577) by the English writer Raphael Holinshed (d. ?1580) as the incubus of Dame Alice Kyteler, who was condemned as a witch on 2 July 1324. Holinshed explains that "she was charged to haue nightly conference with a spirit called Robert Artisson, to whom she sacrificed in the high way ix red cockes, & ix peacocks eies."

As Yeats explained in his 1934 Introduction to *The Resurrection*, Ptolemy, a second-century astronomer, "thought that the precession of the equinoxes moved at the rate of a degree every hundred years, and that somewhere about the time of Christ and Caesar the equinoctial sun had returned to its original place in the constellations, completing and recommencing the thirty-six thousand years, or three hundred and sixty incarnations of a hundred years apiece, of Plato's Man of Ur [Er]. Hitherto almost every philosopher had some different measure for the Greatest Year, but this Platonic Year, as it was called, soon displaced all others . . ."

TWO SONGS FROM A PLAY

The play was first published in *The Adelphi* (June 1927).

AMONG SCHOOL CHILDREN—Stanza III

Porphyry (232/3–ca. 305) was a Neoplatonic philosopher. Yeats would have known his *De Antro Nympharum* in the paraphrase translation by the English scholar Thomas Taylor (1758–1835), "Concerning the Cave of the Nymphs," first published ca. 1788 and included in Taylor's *Select Works* (1823). Prophyry notes that honey "aptly represents the pleasure and delight of descending into the fascinating realms of generation." Taylor also quotes from the commentary on Marcus Tullius Cicero's *Somnium Sciponis* (*Scipio's Dream*) by the fifth-century Neoplatonist Macrobius: "As soon, therefore, as the soul gravitates towards body, in this first production of herself, she begins to experience a material tumult, that is, matter flowing into her essence. And this is what Plato remarks in the Phaedo, that the soul is drawn into the body, staggering with recent intoxication, signifying by this the new drink of matter's impetuous flood, through which the soul becoming defiled and heavy, is drawn into a terrene situation. But the starry *cup,* placed between Cancer and Lion, is a symbol of this mystic truth, signifying that descending souls first experience intoxication in that part of the heavens, through the influx of matter."

THE GIFT OF HARUN AL-RASHID

For Kusta ben Luka, see editorial note to "The Gift of Harun Al-Rashid" (pp. 128–32). For Ahern[e] and Robartes, see Yeats's 1922 note quoted in the editorial note to "Owen Ahern and His Dancers" (p. 127). By the time of *A Vision,* John Aherne had been subsumed back into Owen Aherne.

NOTES TO THE POEMS

SAILING TO BYZANTIUM

First published *October Blast* (1927), including Yeats's note (p. 105). Included without the note in *Stories of Red Hanrahan and The Secret Rose* (1927).

In *A Vision* (1925), Yeats described the Byzantium of the early sixth century as virtually an ideal city: "I think that in early Byzantium, and maybe never before or since in recorded history, religious, aesthetic and practical life were one, and that architect and artificers—though not, it may be, poets, for language had been the instrument of controversy and must have grown abstract—spoke to the multitude and the few alike. The painter and the mosaic worker, the worker in gold and silver, the illuminator of Sacred Books were almost impersonal, almost perhaps without the consciousness of individual design, absorbed in their subject matter and that the vision of a whole people. They could copy out of old Gospel books those pictures that seemed as sacred as the text, and yet weave all into a vast design, the work of many that seemed the work of one, that made building, picture, pattern, metal work of rail and lamp, seem but a single image; and this vision, this proclamation of their invisible master had the Greek nobility, Satan always the still half divine Serpent, never the horned scarecrow of the didactic Middle Ages."

19: to perne is to move in a circular, spinning motion; a gyre is one of the two interlocked cones that Yeats used in *A Vision* and elsewhere to represent the rise and fall of civiliza-

117

118   NOTES TO THE POEMS

tions. The basic meaning of "perne in a gyre" is thus to reenter the world of time and of conflict. 27–29: see Yeats's note, p. 105.

THE TOWER

First published *The Criterion* (June 1927) and *The New Republic* (29 June 1927). Included in *October Blast* (1927) with Yeats's note (pp. 105–6).

11: in Greek mythology, the Nine Muses are the goddesses of the arts; Yeats is perhaps thinking of Erato, the goddess of love poetry. 12: Plato (ca. 428–ca. 347 B.C.), Greek philosopher; Plotinus (205–270), Roman Neoplatonic philosopher, possibly born in Egypt. 25–32: see Yeats's note, p. 105. 33–48: see Yeats's note, p. 105. Cloone Bog is in County Galway, near Gort. 52: the Greek poet Homer (ca. eighth century B.C.) is traditionally thought to have been blind. 53: the abduction of Helen by Paris was the cause of the Trojan War. 57–72: see Yeats's note, p. 105. 65: a bawn (*bán*) is a pasture or yard, sometimes fortified; but in Yeats's "Red Hanrahan" the event described occurs in a barn. 80: see Yeats's note, p. 105, for the "ancient bankrupt master." 85: Yeats discusses the "Great Memory passing on from generation to generation" in the "Anima Mundi" section of his *Per Amica Silentia Lunae* (1918); essentially, it is a repository of archetypal images. 114: Hanrahan's life is dominated by a vain search to recover his vision of Echtge, a fairy goddess. 132: Edmund Burke (1729–97), Irish writer and orator; Henry Grattan (1746–1820), Irish political leader. 136: in Greek mythology, the horns of Amalthea, the goat that nursed Zeus (the ruler of the Olympian gods), flowed with nectar and ambrosia; one of them broke off and was given to Zeus. The cornucopia thus became a symbol of plenty. 140–44: see Yeats's note, p. 106. Traditionally, a swan sings only in the moments before its death. 146–47: see Yeats's note, p. 107. 156: a paradise beyond the moon and thus presumably timeless. 181: compose one's soul, particularly in preparation for death.

MEDITATIONS IN TIME OF CIVIL WAR

First published *The London Mercury* (January 1923) and *The Dial* (January 1923). Included with Yeats's notes (pp. 108–9) in *The Cat and the Moon and Certain Poems* (1924).

I.9: the Greek poet Homer (ca. eighth century B.C.). I.27: in Roman mythology, Juno is queen of the gods and a protector of women. II.1: the poem is set at Thoor Ballylee (see Yeats's note to "The Tower," p. 105). II.14: title character of "Il Penseroso" (1632) by the English poet John Milton (1608–74). III.2: Junzo Sato presented Yeats with a ceremonial Japanese sword in March 1920. III.8: the English poet Geoffrey Chaucer (d. 1400) was born ca. 1340. III.32: as a symbol of immortality, the peacock was sacred to Juno. In *A Vision* (1925), Yeats refers to the peacock's scream as heralding the end of a civilization. IV.3: Anne Yeats (1919–2001); Michael Butler Yeats (1921–). IV.17: in Ptolemaic astronomy, the Primum Mobile is the outermost concentric sphere, carrying the spheres of the fixed stars and the planets in its daily revolution. IV.21: Lady Gregory (1852–1932), Yeats's close friend and collaborator. IV.22: Bertha Georgie Hyde-Lees (1892–1968), whom Yeats married on 20 October 1917. V.1–5: see Yeats's note, p. 108. The Irregulars were members of the Irish Republican Army. V.2: Falstaff is a comic character in several plays by the English playwright William Shakespeare (1564–1616). V.6: members of the army of the Free State government. VI.5: see Yeats's note, p. 108. VII.9–10: see Yeats's note, p. 108. VII.20: Babylon was an ancient city in Mesopotamia. Yeats was familiar with Babylonian astrology, referring in *A Vision* (1925) to the "mathematical Babylonian starlight." VII.29: see Yeats's note, p. 109.

NINETEEN HUNDRED AND NINETEEN

First published *The Dial* (September 1921) and *The London Mercury* (November 1921) as "Thoughts upon the Present

State of the World," with Yeats's note, p. 109. Included in
Seven Poems and a Fragment (1922).

During the course of 1919, armed conflicts between the
English-controlled government of Ireland and the Irish
Republican Army became more frequent.

I.6: probably the olive-wood statue of Athena Polias in the
Erechtheum, one of the central buildings (constructed
421–407 B.C.) in the Athenian Acropolis. **I.7:** Phidias (ca.
490–ca. 432 B.C.), Athenian sculptor, best known for his chrys-
elephantine statues of Athena and Zeus. **I.8:** in the *History of
the Peloponnesian War*, the Greek historian Thucydides (ca.
455–ca. 400 B.C.) mentions the Athenian fashion of "fastening
up the hair in a knot held by a golden grasshopper as brooch."
The bees may derive from the chapter on "The Heroic Age in
Greek Art" in *Greek Studies: A Series of Essays* (1895) by the
English writer Walter Pater (1839–94), which mentions "the
golden honeycomb of Daedalus." In the texts of the poem
prior to *The Tower*, both artifacts were ascribed to Phidias
("his golden grasshoppers and bees"). **I.19–20:** see Isaiah 2:4—
"And they shall beat their swords into plowshares and their
spears into pruninghooks; nation shall not lift up sword against
nation, neither shall they learn war any more." **II.1:** Loïe
Fuller (1862–1928), an American dancer best known for her
"Serpentine Dance," first performed in February 1892. Her
dancers were Japanese, not Chinese. **II.6:** see Yeats's note,
p. 109. **III.1:** most likely the English poet Percy Bysshe Shel-
ley (1792–1822), who writes in *Prometheus Unbound* (1820),
"My soul is like an enchanted boat / Which, like a sleeping
swan, doth float / Upon the silver waves." **III.14–16:** probably
Thomas Taylor (see Yeats's note to "Among School Children,"
p. 110). In *De Antro Nympharum* Taylor explains that after
departed souls have passed the Stygian river, "they are entirely
ignorant of their pristine life on earth. . . . However, by means
of the blood, departed spirits recognize material forms, and
recollect their pristine condition on the earth." **VI.1:** see
Yeats's note, p. 109. **VI.6:** in his note to "The Hosting of the

Sidhe" (1893), first published in *The Wind Among the Reeds* (1899), Yeats explained that the Sidhe "journey in whirling wind, the winds that were called the dance of the daughters of Herodias in the Middle Ages, Herodias doubtless taking the place of some old goddess." Herodias is a witch-goddess in Germanic mythology. Yeats probably read about her in *Teutonic Mythology* (trans. J. S. Stallybrass, 1883–88) by the German folklorist Jacob Grimm (1785–1863). Grimm explains that "quite early in the Mid. Ages the Christian mythus of Herodias got mixed up with our native heathen fables; those notions about dame Holda and the 'furious host' and the nightly jaunts of sorceresses were grafted on it, the Jewish king's daughter had the part of a heathen goddess assigned her . . . , and her worship found numerous adherents. In the same circle moves Diana, the lunar deity of night, the wild huntress; Diana, Herodias, and Holda stand for one another, or side by side." Moreover, "to this day" a whirlwind "is accounted for in Lower Saxony (about Celle) by the dancing Herodias whirling about in the air," and "Herodias was dragged into the circle of night-women . . . because she played and danced, and since her death goes booming through the air as the 'wind's bride.'" The name Herodias comes from the story of John the Baptist, who denounced the marriage of Herod Antipas to Herodias, the divorced wife of his half-brother Herod Philip and daughter of his half-brother Aristobulus. During his birthday celebration, Herod Antipas is so impressed by the dancing of Herodias' daughter by Herod Philip that he swears to give her anything she wishes; prompted by her mother, she asks for the head of John the Baptist, who is then killed (Matt. 14:1–12; Mark 6:17–29). In most accounts cited by Grimm, the daughter is also named Herodias; but biblical tradition follows the Greek historian and Jewish priest Flavius Josephus (b. A.D. 37/38) in naming her Salome. VI.16–18: see Yeats's note, p. 109.

THE WHEEL

First published *Seven Poems and a Fragment* (1922).

YOUTH AND AGE

First published *The Cat and the Moon and Certain Poems* (1924).

THE NEW FACES

First published *Seven Poems and a Fragment* (1922).
1: Manuscript evidence indicates that the poem was addressed to Lady Gregory, although Yeats did not offer a note to that effect in any printing.

A PRAYER FOR MY SON

First published *Seven Poems and a Fragment*.
Michael Butler Yeats, born 22 August 1921.
17: "You" is God, seen later in the stanza as Christ. In Christian tradition, the infant Christ is taken to Egypt by the Virgin Mary and her husband, Joseph, to escape the wrath of King Herod, who was afraid of the prophecy that he would be supplanted by Christ (see Matt. 2:1–18).

TWO SONGS FROM A PLAY

First published as part of the play *The Resurrection* in *The Adelphi* (November 1927); first published separately and with Yeats's note, p. 109, in *October Blast* (1927). A fourth stanza was added to the revised version of *The Resurrection* included in *Stories of Michael Robartes and His Friends* (1932) and was also included in the separate version of the poem in the *Collected Poems* (1933):

IV

Everything that man esteems
Endures a moment or a day.
Love's pleasure drives his love away,
The painter's brush consumes his dreams;
The herald's cry, the soldier's tread
Exhaust his glory and his might.
Whatever flames upon the night
Man's own resinous heart has fed.

I.1–8: this stanza recounts the death and, implicitly, the resurrection of Dionysus, the god of wine and fertility in Greek mythology. Though there are varied and sometimes conflicting legends, the essentials are the birth of Dionysus from the god Zeus and a mortal woman; the jealousy of Hera, Zeus' wife, leading to Dionysus being torn to pieces and devoured by the Titans; the saving of his heart by Athena, who carries it to Zeus; and Zeus' swallowing of the heart, leading to the rebirth of Dionysus, in common legend by Semele. I.6: in Greek mythology the nine Muses are the patrons of arts and sciences. I.7: for "Magnus Annus" ("Great Year"), see Yeats's note to "Nineteen Hundred and Nineteen," p. 109. I.9–16: this stanza recounts the birth of Christ through reference to the *Fourth Eclogue* (40 B.C.) of the Roman poet Virgil (70–19 B.C.). At the end of the Golden Age, Astrea, daughter of Zeus and Themis and goddess of justice, withdraws from the earth and is transformed into the constellation Virgo. In a passage that Yeats quotes in *A Vision* (1925), Virgil prophesies the return of Astrea and the start of a new Golden Age. Beginning with the Council of Nicea in 325, the *Fourth Eclogue* was seen as foretelling the birth of Christ, Astrea being equated with the Virgin Mary and the star Spica (Alpha Virginis, the most prominent star in the constellation Virgo) with the Star of Bethlehem. Moreover, in *A Vision* Yeats explains that "the vernal equinox at the birth of Christ" falls between the signs Pisces and Aries in the zodiac and that the sun's "transition from Pisces to Aries had

for generations been associated with the ceremonial death
and resurrection of Dionysus. Near that transition the women
wailed him, and the night showed the full moon separating
from the constellation Virgo, with the star in the wheatsheaf,
or in the child, for in the old maps she is represented carrying
now one now the other." Thus this stanza implicitly parallels
Virgin Mary/Christ not only with Virgo/Spica but also with
Athena/Dionysus. In the *Fourth Eclogue,* Virgil also prophesies
another Trojan War and another journey by Jason and the
Argonauts in search of the Golden Fleece. **I.16**: in *Select Pas-
sages Illustrating Neo-Platonism* (1923), E. R. Dodds explains
that "it was in Plato's city that Greek thought made its last
stand against the Church which it envisaged as 'a fabulous
and formless darkness mastering the loveliness of the world.'"
Dodd is loosely paraphrasing *The Lives of the Sophists* (ca. 396)
by the Greek sophist Eunapius (ca. 347–ca. 420). Writing
about Antoninus (d. ca. 390), son of Eustathius, Eunapius
notes that "he foretold to all his followers that after his death
the temple would cease to be, and even the great and holy
temples of Serapis would pass into formless darkness and be
transformed, and that a fabulous and unseemly gloom would
hold sway over the fairest things on earth. To all these prophe-
cies time bore witness, and in the end his prediction gained
the force of an oracle." **II.2**: in *The Resurrection,* "that room" is
the site of Christ's Last Supper. **II.3**: Galilee, a region in Pales-
tine, was the chief scene of the ministry of Christ. **II.4**: for
"Babylonian starlight," see note above to "Meditations in
Time of Civil War," **VII.20** (p. 117). **II.7–8**: the classical world
as epitomized by the philosophy of Plato and the Doric style of
architecture.

WISDOM

First published *October Blast* (1927).
    7: Joseph, husband of the Virgin Mary. **11**: the Virgin Mary,
mother of Christ. **13**: Christ. **14**: for Babylon, see note above to

"Meditations in Time of Civil War," VII.20 (p. 117). **15:** in biblical tradition, the Flood covered the entire world; only Noah and those on board the Ark survived (Gen. 6:5–7:19). **16–17:** an allegorical account of the incarnation of Christ by God through the Virgin Mary.

LEDA AND THE SWAN

First published *The Dial* for June 1924 and *To-morrow* (Dublin) for August 1924. Included in *The Cat and the Moon and Certain Poems* (1924) and *A Vision* (1925). In *The Dial*, Yeats explained,

I wrote Leda and the Swan because the editor of a political review asked me for a poem. I thought, 'After the individualist, demagogic movement, founded by Hobbes and popularized by the Encyclopaedists and the French revolution, we have a soil so exhausted that it cannot grow that crop again for centuries.' Then I thought, 'Nothing is now possible but some movement from above preceded by some violent annunciation.' My fancy began to play with Leda and the Swan for metaphor, and I began this poem; but as I wrote, bird and lady took such possession of the scene that all politics went out of it, and my friend tells me that his 'conservative readers would misunderstand the poem.'

Yeats refers to his friend the Irish writer and painter George W. Russell (AE, 1867–1935), who became editor of the *Irish Statesman* in 1923. Thomas Hobbes (1588–1679) was an English philosopher. The Encyclopaedists were the group of writers who produced the French *Encyclopédie* (1751–72; supplement 1776–77), a major factor in the development of the French Revolution of 1789–99.

In classical mythology, the god Zeus comes to the mortal Leda in the form of a swan. The result of that union varies in different accounts. A typescript for *A Vision* (1925) suggests

that at the time Yeats was following the version in which Zeus is the father of Helen and the Dioscuri (Castor and Polydeuces), but Tyndareus (Leda's husband) is the father of Clytemnestra. By the second edition of *A Vision* (1937), Yeats followed the version in which Zeus is the father of all four children. The abduction of Helen by Paris caused the Trojan War and the eventual destruction of Troy. The Greek forces were commanded by Agamemnon, brother of Menelaus, Helen's first husband. On his return from the war, Agamemnon is murdered by Aegisthus, lover of his wife, Clytemnestra.

ON A PICTURE OF A BLACK CENTAUR
BY EDMUND DULAC

First published *Seven Poems and a Fragment* (1922) as "Suggested by a Picture of a Black Centaur."

Edmund Dulac (1882–1953) was an English artist and illustrator and friend of Yeats; no such picture by him has been traced. The Irish artist Cecil ffrench Salkeld (1904–69) once claimed that the poem was inspired by a watercolor of his; Mrs. Yeats is said to have explained that the poem was begun in relation to a picture by Dulac but altered in relation to Salkeld's. In Greek mythology, the Centaurs are usually depicted as having the upper part of a human body and the lower body of a horse.

7: describing a particular variety of wheat in *A Popular Account of the Ancient Egyptians* (1854), J. Gardner Wilkinson explains that "this is the kind which has been lately grown in England, and which is *said* to have been raised from grains found in the tombs of Thebes." **11–12**: in Christian legend, seven martyrs were immured in a cave near the ancient city of Ephesus during the persecution by Decius (d. 251). Two centuries later they awoke and were taken before Theodosius II (401–450), their story confirming his wavering faith. Alexander the Great (356–323 B.C.) captured Ephesus in 334 B.C.; his empire quickly dissolved after his death.

AMONG SCHOOL CHILDREN

First published *The London Mercury* (August 1927) and *The Dial* (August 1927). Included in *October Blast* (1927) with Yeats's note, p. 110.

I.1–2: in his capacity as a member of the Irish Senate, Yeats visited St. Otteran's School, Waterford, in February 1926. The "kind old nun" was the Reverend Mother Philomena, the Mistress of Schools. **II.1**: see note above to "Leda and the Swan," pp. 123–24. From a biographical perspective, the "Ledaean body" refers to Maud Gonne (1866–1953), Yeats's first beloved. Yeats wrote to Gonne on 13 June 1928: "I send a fresh copy of my book. You will find a reference to your self in 'Among School Children'—a Waterford School I went over—I do not think it will offend you. The book seems to me the best I have done, it is certainly the most successful." (*The Gonne-Yeats Letters 1893–1938*, ed. Anna MacBride White and A. Norman Jeffares [New York and London: Norton, 1993], 445.) **II.7–8**: in Plato's *Symposium*, the Greek playwright Aristophanes (ca. 450–ca. 385 B.C.) argues that primal man was double, in a nearly spherical shape, until Zeus divided him into two, as a cooked egg divided by a hair. Love is seen as an attempt to recover the lost unity. **IV.2**: an artist of fifteenth-century Italy (the text in *The London Mercury* reads "Da Vinci' finger," referring to Leonardo da Vinci [1452–1519]). **V.2**: see Yeats's note, p. 110. **VI.1**: Plato (ca. 429–347 B.C.), Greek philosopher. **VI.3**: Aristotle (384–322 B.C.), Greek philosopher, here depicted as tutor to Alexander the Great. **VI.5**: Pythagoras (ca. 582–ca. 507 B.C.), Greek philosopher, discover of the mathematical basis of musical intervals; the detail of his golden thigh is reported by Iamblichus in his *Life of Pythagoras*. **VI.7**: for the Muses, see note above to "Two Songs from a Play," I.1–8 (p. 121).

COLONUS' PRAISE

First published *The Tower* (1928). A chorus from Yeats's translation of *Oedipus at Colonus* by the Greek playwright Sophocles (ca. 496–406 B.C.). The full text of Yeats's version was not published until the *Collected Plays* (1934).

1: Colonus, a district just north of Athens, was connected with horses because of the worship there of the god Poseidon, who gave the gift of horses to men. 8: "Semele's lad" is Dionysus. See note above to "Two Songs from a Play," I.1–8 (p. 121). 9–16: the "gymnasts' garden" is the Academy, a park and gymnasium on the outskirts of Athens, adjoining Colonus, and the site of the school founded by Plato ca. 385 B.C. The olive was the gift of the goddess Athena to mankind; an olive in the Academy is said to have sprung up next after the primal olive (near the west end of the Erechtheum on the Acropolis). 19: the "Great Mother" is Demeter, a corn goddess in Greek mythology; her daughter, Persephone, is carried off into the underworld by Hades. 23: a river flowing past the west side of Athens. 28: Poseidon taught men to row as well as to ride.

THE HERO, THE GIRL, AND THE FOOL

First published *Seven Poems and a Fragment* (1922) as "Cuchulain the Girl and the Fool," Cuchulain (*Cú Chulainn*, "The Hound of Culann") being the central figure of the Ulster cycle of heroic tales. Lines 18–29 only were included in *A Vision* (1925) as "The Fool by the Roadside." The shorter form was also used in the *Collected Poems* (1933).

OWEN AHERN AND HIS DANCERS

First published as two separate poems, "The Lover Speaks" and "The Heart Replies," in *The Dial* (June 1924). Included in that same format in *The Cat and the Moon and Certain Poems* (1924). In a note first published in *Later Poems* (1922) to "The

Phases of the Moon" and "The Double Vision of Michael Robartes" (included in *The Wild Swans at Coole*, 1919) and to "Michael Robartes and the Dancer" (included in *Michael Robartes and the Dancer*, 1921), Yeats explained:

Years ago I wrote three stories in which occurs the names of Michael Robartes and Owen Aherne. I now consider that I used the actual names of two friends, and that one of these friends, Michael Robartes, has but lately returned from Mesopotamia where he has partly found and partly thought out much philosophy. I consider that John Aherne is either the original Aherne or some near relation of the man that was, and that both he and Robartes, to whose namesake I had attributed a turbulent life and death, have quarrelled with me. They take their place in a phantasmagoria in which I endeavour to explain my philosophy of life and death, and till that philosophy has found some detailed exposition in prose certain passages in the poems named above may seem obscure. To some extent I wrote them as a text for exposition.

Michael Robartes and Owen Aherne are depicted in the stories "Rosa Alchemica" (1896), "The Tables of the Law" (1896), and "The Adoration of the Magi" (1897), and they reappear in *A Vision* (1925).

I.2: Normandy, a region in France. II.2–4: if the poem is read biographically, the "young child" is Iseult Gonne (1895–1954), daughter of Maud Gonne; and the female "cage bird" is Georgie Hyde-Lees (1892–1968), whom Yeats married on 20 October 1917. Yeats had proposed to Iseult on 7 August 1917 while staying with her and Maud in Maud's cottage in Normandy but was refused.

A MAN YOUNG AND OLD

VI, VII, VIII, and X first published as "More Songs from an Old Countryman" in *The London Mercury* (April 1926). I–IV

first published as "Four Songs from the Young Countryman" and V and IX as "Two Songs from the Old Countryman" in *The London Mercury* (May 1927). Included in *October Blast* under the titles "The Young Countryman" (I–IV) and "The Old Countryman" (V–X). Prior to *The Tower* (1928) the poems were numbered but not given individual titles.

VI.5: Hector is killed by Achilles in the Trojan War. **VI.15**: "she" is Helen of Troy. **X.3**: the abduction of Helen by Paris caused the Trojan War.

THE THREE MONUMENTS

First published *October Blast* (1927).

Monuments on O'Connell Street in Dublin to the English hero Horatio Nelson (1758–1805) and the Irish political leaders Daniel O'Connell (1775–1847) and Charles Stewart Parnell (1846–91). Nelson's Pillar, between the others, was the tallest of the three.

FROM 'OEDIPUS AT COLONUS'

First published *October Blast* (1927). A chorus from Yeats's translation of *Oedipus at Colonus* by the Greek playwright Sophocles (ca. 496–406 B.C.). The full text of Yeats's version was not published until the *Collected Plays* (1934).

VI.6: Oedipus and his daughters, Antigone and Ismene.

THE GIFT OF HARUN AL-RASHID

First published *English Life and The Illustrated Review* (January 1924) and *The Dial* (June 1924). Included in *The Cat and the Moon and Certain Poems* (1924) and *A Vision* (1925), in the latter as "Desert Geometry or The Gift of Harun Al-Raschid." Yeats's note in *The Tower* (p. 110) was published for the first time.

In his note to the poem in *The Dial* (June 1924) and *The Cat and the Moon and Certain Poems* (1924), Yeats explained:

This poem is founded on the following passages in a letter of Owen Ahern's, which I am publishing in 'A Vision.'

'After the murder for an unknown reason of Jaffer, head of the family of the Barmecides, Harun-al-Rashid seemed as though a great weight had fallen from him, and in the rejoicing of the moment, a rejoicing that seemed to Jaffar's friends a disguise for his remorse, he brought a new bride into the house. Wishing to confer an equal happiness upon his friend, he chose a young bride for Kusta-ben-Luka. According to one tradition of the desert, she had, to the great surprise of her friends, fallen in love with the elderly philosopher, but according to another Harun bought her from a passing merchant. Kusta, a christian like the Caliph's own physician, had planned, one version of the story says, to end his days in a Monastery at Nisibis, while another story has it that he was deep in a violent love affair that he had arranged for himself. The only thing upon which there is general agreement is that he was warned by a dream to accept the gift of the Caliph, and that his wife a few days after the marriage began to talk in her sleep, and that she told him all those things which he had searched for vainly all his life in the great library of the Caliph and in the conversation of wise men. One curious detail has come down to us in Bedouin tradition. When awake she was a merry girl with no more interest in matters of the kind than other girls of her age, and Kusta, the apple of whose eye she had grown to be, fearing that it would make her think his love but self-interest, never told her that she talked to him in her sleep. Michael Robartes frequently heard Bedouins quoting this as proof of Kusta-ben-Luka's extraordinary wisdom . . . . even in the other world Kusta's bride is supposed to remain in ignorance of her share in founding the religion of the Judwalis, and for this reason young girls, who think themselves wise, are

ordered by their fathers and mothers to wear little amulets on which her name has been written. All these contradictory stories seem to be a confused recollection of the contents of a little old book, lost many years ago with Kusta-ben-Luka's larger book, in the desert battle which I have already described. This little book was discovered according to tradition, by some Judwali scholar or saint, between the pages of a greek book which had once been in the Caliph's library. The story of the discovery may however be the invention of a much later age to justify some doctrine, or development of old doctrine, that it may have contained.'

In my poem I have greatly elaborated this bare narrative, but I do not think it too great a poetical license to describe Kusta as hesitating between the poems of Sappho and the treatise of Parmenides as hiding places. Gibbon says the poems of Sappho were still extant in the twelfth century, and it does not seem impossible that a great philosophical work, of which we possess only fragments, may have found its way into an Arab library of the eighth century. Certainly there are passages of Parmenides, that for instance numbered one hundred and thirty by Burkitt, and still more in his immediate predecessors, which Kusta would have recognised as his own thought. This from Herakleitus for instance "Mortals are Immortals and Immortals are Mortals, the one living the other's death and dying the other's life."

For Ahern[e] and Robartes, see above note to "Owen Ahern and His Dancers," p. 127; the letter was not included in *A Vision* (1925). Harun al-Rashid (766–809) was caliph of Baghdad from 786 until his death. The Baramika was an Iranian family of secretaries and viziers to the Abbasid caliphs. Yahya was vizier from 786 to 803, when Harun al-Rashid imprisoned him and one of his sons, executing his other son, Dja'far, who had been the caliph's favorite. Kusta ben Luka (d. ca. 912/913) was a

doctor and translator. Nisbis, in Syria, was the ancient resi-
dence of Bedouin kings; the Bedouin, Arabic for "tent
dwellers," were the nomad peoples of interior Arabia. Yeats
invented the tribe of Judwalis ("Diagrammatists"). In *A Vision*
(1925), Michael Robartes explains that "The Judwali had once
possessed a learned book called 'The Way of the Soul between
the Sun and the Moon' and attributed to a certain Kusta ben
Luka, Christian Philosopher at the Court of Harun Al-Raschid,
and . . . this, and a smaller book describing the personal life of
the philosopher, had been lost or destroyed in desert fighting."

Sappho (ca. 612 B.C.–?) was a Greek poet. In *The History of
the Decline and Fall of the Roman Empire* (1776–88), the English
historian Edward Gibbon (1737–94) noted that her works were
still studied in the twelfth century. Parmenides (ca. 541 B.C.–?)
and Heraclitus (ca. 535–ca. 475 B.C.) were Greek philosophers.
Yeats refers to *Early Greek Philosophy* (1892) by the Scottish
scholar John Burnet (1863–1928). In his own copy Yeats
marked this passages from Parmenides, lines 127–132 ("130" is
the marginal line number): "The narrower circles are filled
with unmixed fire, and those surrounding them with night,
and in the midst of these rushes their portion of fire. In the
midst of these circles is the divinity that directs the course of
all things; for she rules over all painful birth and all begetting,
driving the female to the embrace of the male, and the male to
that of the female. First of all the gods she contrived Eros."
Yeats also marked this passage from Heraclitus (Fragment 67
in Burnet's numbering) in his copy of *Early Greek Philosophy*:
"Mortals are immortals and immortals are mortals, the one liv-
ing the other's death and dying the other's life."

From a biographical perspective, "The Gift of Harun Al-
Rashid" is a veiled tribute to the automatic writing and
"sleeps" of Mrs. Yeats that provided the materials for *A Vision*.

2: Abd Al-Rabban, called "Faristah" in the first printing of
the poem, has not been traced. **6**: in a note included in *The Dial*
(June 1924) and *The Cat and the Moon and Certain Poems*
(1924), Yeats explained, "The banners of the Abbasid Caliphs

were black as an act of mourning for those who had fallen in battle at the establishment of the dynasty." The Abbasid caliphs ruled from 750 to 1258. The first printing of the poem had referred to the "gold embroidered banners of the Calif." **135**: a djinn is a supernatural being who can be either benevolent or malicious. **184**: in a note to this line published only in *The Dial* (June 1924), Yeats explained that "All those gyres and cubes and midnight things" "refers to the geometrical forms which Robartes describes the Judwali Arabs as making upon the sand for the instruction of their young people, and which, according to tradition, were drawn as described in sleep by the wife of Kusta-ben-Luka."

ALL SOULS' NIGHT

First published *The London Mercury* (March 1921) and *The New Republic* (9 March 1921). Included in *Seven Poems and a Fragment* (1922) and *A Vision* (1925). Subtitle first used in *The Tower* (1928).

In the Roman Catholic Church, All Souls' Day (usually 2 November) is the feast in which the church on earth prays for the souls of all the faithful departed still suffering in Purgatory. **1**: Christ Church, one of the colleges of Oxford University. **21**: "Horton's" in the *Collected Poems* (1933). William Thomas Horton (1864–1919), English mystical painter and illustrator. **25**: Amy Audrey Locke (1881–1916), Horton's beloved, with whom he enjoyed a platonic relationship. **41**: Florence Farr (Mrs. Edward Emery, 1869–1917), English actress. **46–50**: Farr left England in September 1912 to teach in Ceylon. **53**: probably Sir Ponnambalam Ramanathan (1851–1930), who founded the school where Farr taught. **61**: MacGregor Mathers (1854–1918), occultist and one of the founders of the Order of the Golden Dawn, which Yeats joined on 7 March 1890. Yeats and Mathers became estranged after a quarrel over Order matters in 1900.

DATE DUE

THE FIRST EDITION OF
W. B. Yeats's *The Tower* appeared in bookstores in
London on Valentine's Day, 1928. His English pub-
lisher printed just 2,000 copies of this slender volume
of twenty-one poems, priced at six shillings. The
book was immediately embraced by book buyers and
critics alike, and it quickly became a bestseller.

Subsequent versions of the volume made various
changes throughout, but this Scribner facsimile
edition reproduces exactly that seminal first edition
as it reached its earliest audience in 1928, adding an
introduction and notes by esteemed Yeats scholar
Richard J. Finneran.

Written between 1912 and 1927, these poems
("Sailing to Byzantium," "Leda and the Swan," and
"Among School Children" among them) are today
considered some of the best and most famous in the
entire Yeats canon. As Virginia Woolf declared in her
unsigned review of this collection, "Mr. Yeats has
never written more exactly and more passionately."

SCRIBNER
Cover design by Alese Pickering
Cover illustration by John Pireman, based
  upon original cover art by T. Sturge Moore
Register online at www.simonsays.com for more
information on this and other great books.

U.S. $14.00
Can. $18.99   0104

ISBN 978-0-7432-4728-3

51400

9 780743 247283

P9-EAF-236